Dr. MARIA BARRIOS

BEING CONSCIOUS

Think, feel and act to achieve your goals

BEING CONSCIOUS

First edition: January, 2023.

Text copyright ©2021, Dr. Maria Barrios.

Art copyright ©2021, Ordinal, S.A. de C.V. / Ordinal LLC

www.ordinalbooks.com

contacto@ordinalbooks.com

ISBN: 978-607-59545-3-0

*To all the brave people who are
building their lives by design and
not by default.*

*Thanks to my parents for
the gift of life, which is the
greatest privilege.*

This book aims to help you develop your consciousness. According to a study published in the Harvard Business Review1, only between 10 and 15% of the people are self-aware, despite the fact that the most self-aware earn $29,000 more per year and are 69% more likely to be successful.

INTRODUCTION

The ultimate goal of all human beings is fulfillment or wholeness. Happiness comes and goes; it depends on what happens outside. Fulfillment comes from within, is built over time and can be expressed in many ways. Most commonly, fulfillment is sought in terms of health, money, or love. In whatever way we are looking for that wholeness, it will be easier to experience it if we know ourselves, if we know how our mind works.

Let's think of a clock. If we had never seen one, we might believe that the movement of the hands is magic. In the same way, when we look at a person with money, someone with a good relationship or with an athletic body, we think that they were born with a gift or that it is luck. The truth is that luck and magic are built.

Everything can be created, but first we
need to know how we work in order to
then achieve what we want.

To understand how to create the conditions that will lead us to fulfillment, it is necessary to know how to distinguish between **external reality** and **internal reality**. **External reality** could be synonymous with the **laws of nature** (*outside*). And **internal reality** is our inner **interpretation** of what happens outside, which sometimes we can even call distortion.

Outside

We live in a physical world, in which the laws of nature operate—such as the laws of cause and effect or, as Newton's third law puts it, "For every action there is a reaction." Our emotions, like everything related to our body, obey the law of action-consequence—the law of nature.

Each one of our decisions generates
a consequence, even if the decision
is not to *decide.*

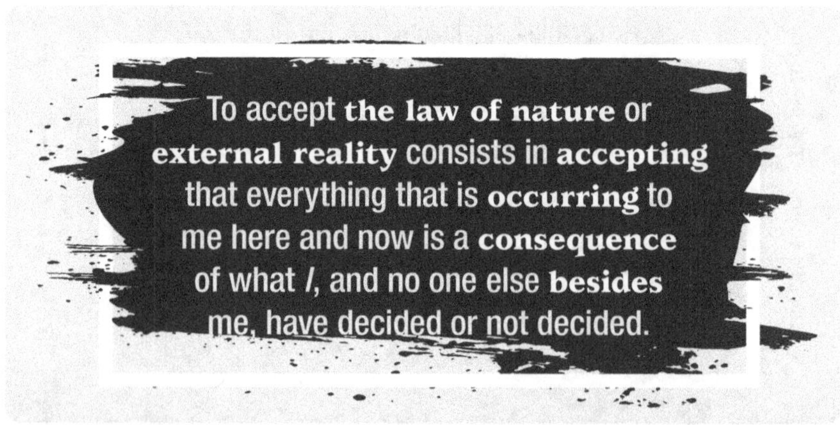

Inside

We are human beings with incredible but limited capabilities. Our brain has a great perceptual border, since it cannot process 100 percent of everything that happens outside. So, what our brain does is trim away some information so as not to become oversaturated.

The instrument that our brain has for trimming down reality is attention. Of everything that happens in external reality, we only retain and process what we pay attention to. It is said that human beings can pay attention to a maximum of five percent of the things happening at any moment, and we repress or simply do not register the other 95 percent.

We try to organize this five percent of information, which we have arbitrarily selected using our attention, in the different *compartments* or shelves that we already have. Each head has totally unique *shelves*, and these are shaped by our beliefs, emotional patterns, traumatic experiences, physical state, culture, and many other factors. In the event that information we are trying to organize does not fit easily on any of our shelves, then we remove it, distort it, or even add information to make it fit, at any cost. When new information does not easily fit with any of our existing shelves, very few human beings will then flexibly expand the shelves.

This five percent, some of which we
have distorted or invented, is what
we call our **inner reality**.

Each one of our perceptions is in itself a distortion. That's why none of us owns the absolute truth. We can only perceive a small part of reality, and often we are more concerned with *fitting* it into our compartments than we are in exploring what is really happening moment by moment.

The *true* secret

The great secret to navigating toward fulfillment is a commitment to engage with external reality, no matter what. The more we develop the ability to accept the laws of cause and effect—that is, the more we can accept our responsibility for causing, consciously or unconsciously, what happens to us—then the more we will have wealth, health and love.

No situation escapes the law of cause and effect. Take disease, for example. Does someone with a chronic condition, such as cancer, cause their own death? Does even cancer fall under the law of cause and effect? If the person is an adult, then the answer is yes. However, this does not mean that the person consciously wanted to die. That person, over time, made or did not make a series of decisions that gradually led them to create emotional states that, after a considerable time, ended up biochemically altering their cells until they reached collapse. Most likely, the person was not even aware that this was happening because they were just engaged with their inner reality, with its distortions and its small fragment of reality. It is not that this person is bad or stupid; it is that, like most of us, they were not taught anything different.

That is why this book aims to help us distinguish external from internal reality and, above all, to give us tools to navigate our lives as committed as we can be to external reality—to the **truth**.

How to create a bridge to travel from one side to another? By learning to transform three things: our beliefs, our emotions and our actions. This bridge is not built magically or in minutes. This is not a "happy meal" that will be ready instantly. This bridge is built through a process that requires considerable effort because it involves, above all, stopping blaming other people and things for what happens to us. It implies a high degree of responsibility. And for that we need to be willing to break through our fears, to have a lot of humility, to open our minds and hearts to listen. It implies a great love and appreciation for life. It implies firm and great commitment to live a life by design and not a life by *default*—to be proactive and not victims.

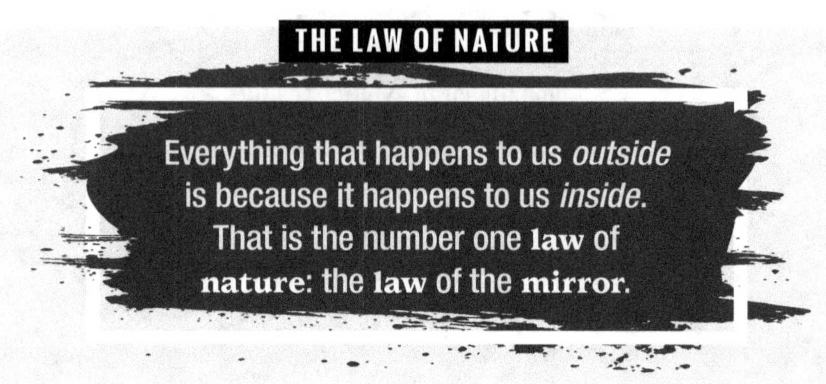

If you are ready to take control of your life and create for yourselves the fulfillment that we have dreamed of and deserve, this book is for you. Here we will learn how to transform our beliefs through **reflective thinking**, how to modify our **emotions**, and how to change our **actions**.

This book has three thematic columns that make up a process to bring us closer to fulfillment, compassion, and our evolution as human beings. The first two chapters give us an introduction to the basic concepts that we will use throughout the process. Then the system will be developed as follows:

REFLECTIVE THOUGHT	EMOTIONS	ACTION
Chapter 3	Chapter 4	Chapter 5
Chapter 6	Chapter 7	Chapter 8
Chapter 9	Chapter 10	Chapter 11
Story that illustrates the theme of reflective thought	Story that illustrates the theme of emotions	Story that illustrates the theme of action

Each chapter is accompanied by a short story that illustrates the topic and an activity that invites us to put what we have learned into practice. Welcome. Enjoy.

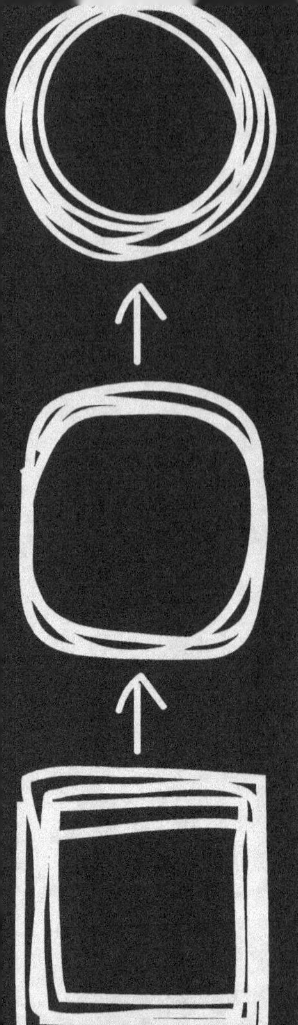

1

TRANSFORM
YOUR MIND

Human beings are the only animals that need to learn to think to survive. and think *consciously*. Any other animal is guided by their instincts: if they are hungry, they go out to look for food; if they perceive danger, they decide between fleeing or fighting. In general, in order to survive, they do not need to analyze consciously the situation in which they find themselves.

Unlike most animals, once we are adults we need to be aware of the different situations in which we find ourselves not only in order to be victorious, but sometimes just to survive. For example, when we are in traffic and another car almost makes us crash, the first natural feeling we have is fear, as our body fires a good rush of adrenaline and cortisol. If we don't stop for a bit to become aware of what just happened and our body's reaction, we could follow our impulse, follow the adrenaline and come to blows with the driver of the other car. If it turns out that the driver of the other car is stronger and more violent than us, or if he brought a weapon, we could put ourselves in grave danger if we only react to our impulse and don't **think** consciously before acting.

If we don't learn to think *consciously*, and only react according to the impulse of the moment, our survival would be threatened. We might break the trust of a relationship by uttering some phrase we didn't think about or risk our inheritance in some business we didn't analyze well, for example.

To learn to think consciously
is a matter of survival.

Small brains and big brains

The theory of the triune brain, proposed by Paul MacLean in the 1960s, explains the human brain by dividing it into three main regions, with distinct functions:

- **The human brain or neocortex**: This is found principally in the most external and frontal part of the head, and is the primordial zone for "thinking well." In this area, primordial processes of analysis, reflection and learning are carried out. The brain is the organ that consumes the most energy, even in repose, and the neocortex is the most demanding of all these three regions.

- **Mammal or limbic brain**: This is found in the central area, in a deeper layer than the neocortex. In this zone, many of our emotions and affections are processed.

- **Reptilian brain**: This is the "stem" of the brain and is located in the deepest part, attached to the beginning of the spinal column. It is also called the "survival brain" because in extreme situations, it is the area in which the greatest amount of energy goes to enable the whole body, especially the extremities, to run or fight.

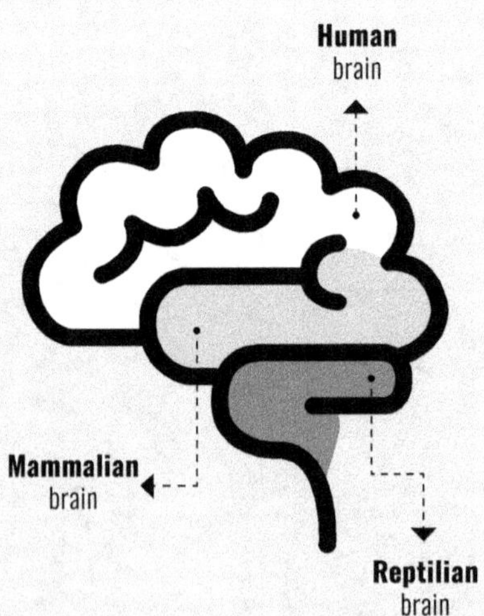

Cycle of consciousness

To learn to think well, one of the first steps is to know how our mind works, because only what is known can be transformed.

Plain and simple, thinking well
is a matter of survival.

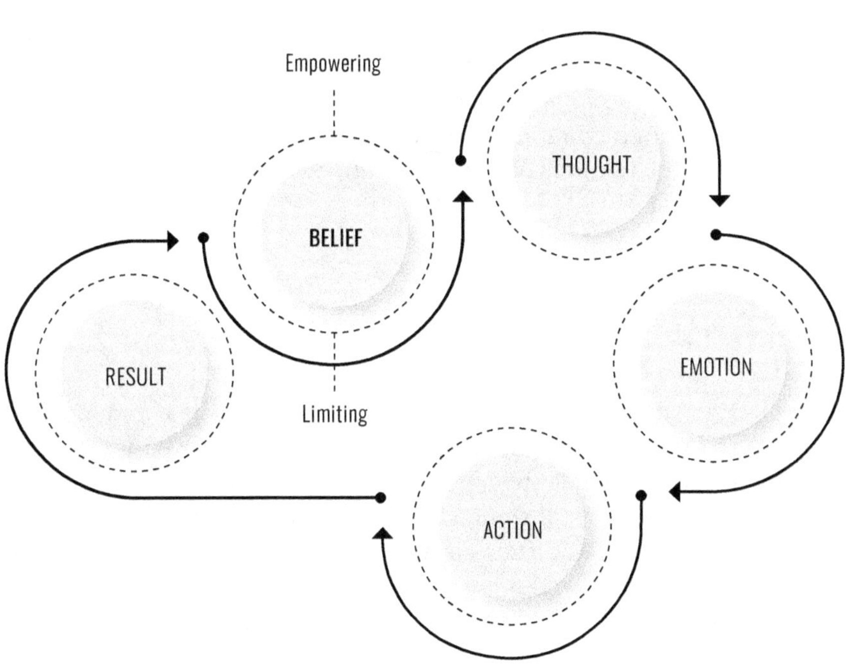

If we were clocks, knowing our *bio-psycho-emotional* mechanism, as shown in the diagram on the preceding page, would be equivalent to understanding the internal gears that permit our machinery to work.

No conduct, from any human being,
is arbitrary or random. We all
behave due to causes and reasons
that follow this same process.

The engineering of this **cycle of consciousness** is inherent in all humans, whether we are aware of it or not. To understand it better, let's do an exercise—let's analyze it from finish to start, in reverse.

Let us think, for example, of a person who enjoys excellent health and vitality. Let's consider this a successful **outcome**. This person achieved health through a series of **actions** carried out, perhaps over several years. These actions ranged from meditating often, choosing nutritious foods, sleeping the hours that the body requires, fostering healthy relationships (including forgiving) and exercising.

If exercise, diet, sleep, forgiveness, healthy relationships, and meditation are all truly related to health, why doesn't everyone practice them? The reason is that there are people who do not have the optimal **emotional** states to carry out these **actions**. If someone does not eat nutritiously, for example, this may be due to an addiction to carbohydrates, and perhaps having an **emotion**, such as anger, and not giving themselves the opportunity to learn to manage it, only knowing how to repress the anger or project it towards others.

The emotions that allow a person to generate proactive actions are in turn generated by constructive **thoughts** such as: "Even though I don't feel like following my diet today, I choose to eat well" or "It sounds tempting to give myself the day off and then stay up late to finish this report on time, but I'll make the better choice: to move forward today."

Finally, **thought** patterns are a consequence of empowering or limiting **beliefs**. Example of thoughts that are empowering for health are: "**I deserve** optimal health," "**I can** learn to take care of myself, although I have not learned it at home," "Setting limits on my diet does **not restrict my freedom**; instead, it expands my health."

On the other hand, if there is a limiting **belief**, they can turn into a vicious circle For example, "I don't deserve health" can generate a **thought** of "For generations everyone in my family has had diabetes and therefore that is what I deserve." These beliefs lead to **emotions** of anger or sadness, which in turn lead to taking an **action**—not taking care of what you eat or how you sleep. And these actions potentially cause a bad **result**: actually developing diabetes.

When we don't understand how this mental process works, we believe that bad results are magical, or that the results we see in our lives are products of our actions alone. We don't realize that there are three essential components that come before the results: **belief**, **thought** and **emotion**.

Result

A result is *something* that has already manifested itself, and that adds value (or doesn't add value).

It is important to note that we are not talking about positive or negative results. For example, there are people who want revenge or to harm others, and they undertake a "successful" process but with destructive results.

Action

Activity is what we undertake to achieve an end. But beware—not undertaking is also an action. Actions have to do with the physical world. They can be seen. They are not merely abstract intentions.

Emotion

Emotions are energy in motion that occurs in the body. The word comes from the Latin *emotio, -ōnis* and has to do with real and physical movement (not with vibrations of the universe or even esoteric concepts). They happen inside us, they are not spread from the environment. They are measurable biochemically through hormones and neurotransmitters. They are only classified as pleasant or unpleasant.

Thought

Thoughts are electrical impulses in our nervous system. They are ideas that can be true or false. It is said that an average person can have between 60,000 and 120,000 thoughts per day, and that 90 percent of these thoughts are the same as the day before.

Belief

Beliefs are neural pathways caused when the same type of electrical impulse occurs so many times that it ends up generating a neural network. Just like thoughts, beliefs are also ideas, which, whether true or false, are often taken for granted, even without evidence. They are the seeds of any outcome.

There are two types of beliefs: **limiting** and **empowering**. The former lead us to results that do not add value to our lives. The empowering ones, logically, do add value to us and to those around us.

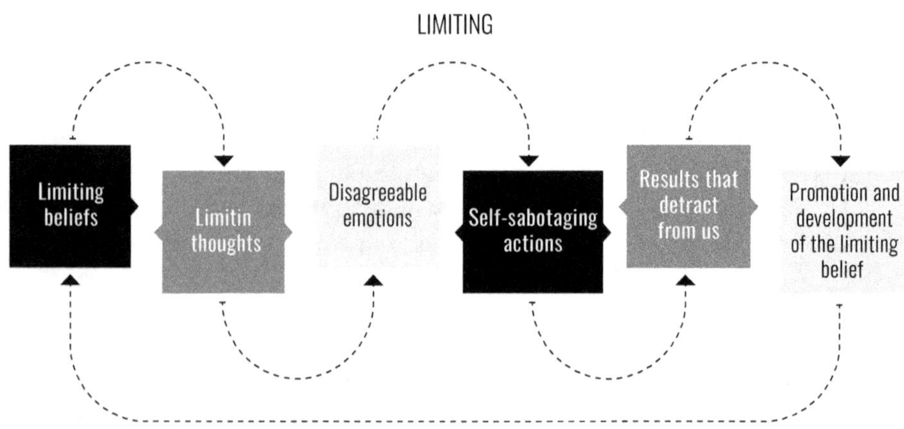

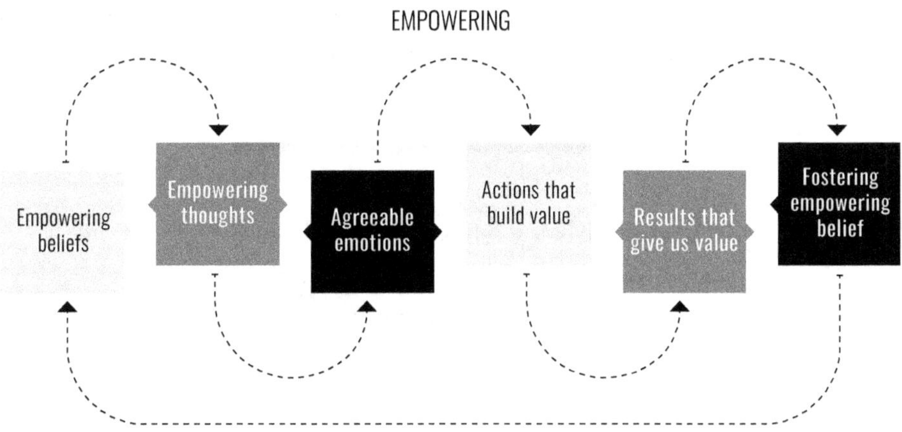

Breaking the vicious circle

Attitude

Many people falsely believe that when someone doesn't achieve the results they expect, the problem is their *attitude* or lack of motivation; That's when the useless advice comes, such as "Get fired up!" or "Yes you can, yes you can!"

Someone can have a lot of good
attitude and at the same time
deep-seated limiting beliefs.

A good attitude (smile, kindness, optimism, etc.), does not necessarily generate a result that adds value.

For example, if in the face of abuse we maintain an inner discourse of "Just ignore it; be optimistic; be kind; always smile; give it a try," we are perpetuating a serious problem, and disguising it with a good attitude.

> Violence is not negotiable. It will not
> end with a smile. You have to start a
> cycle of consciousness to end it.

Extreme events

The cycle of consciousness never stops. We are always believing, thinking, feeling, taking action and getting results. But there could be something that interrupts our cycles: events of extreme pain or extreme pleasure that transform the cycle completely.

An extremely painful event can make a person change their empowering beliefs into limiting ones, and fall into depression, anxiety, and so on. Or, on the other hand, the same painful event can make the person transform their limiting beliefs into empowering ones, and trigger proactive and responsible actions.

Falling in love, for example, produces an altered state of consciousness similar to that of a drugged or drunk person. It breaks the cycle momentarily while the hormones do their job. Then the cycle regains its balance to decide whether to go from falling in love to love, or not.

Two paths

Francisco and Alfredo are twins. They were born with the same genetic information, although with a few grams of difference at birth. They grew up in the same nuclear family and went to the same schools.

Fred, as Alfredo was affectionately called, participated in national track and field competitions, while his brother remained his favorite observer in the front row.

Paco/Paquito—Francisco's nickname changed as he gained weight, until calling him Paquito (Little Paco) became, instead of a tender wink, a mockery of his size.

Paquito and Fred went to college; the former suspended his international tourism career to explore the family's kitchen-sink business. He suddenly married three months into a relationship with his third girlfriend, after the second one left him "for being fat." Days before the wedding, Paco was diagnosed with high blood pressure.

Fred, meanwhile, after two years of introspection, bravely came out of the closet. He ate a healthy diet, and regularly practiced a morning exercise routine. He was 24 years old when he was appointed account manager of a multinational company.

Meanwhile, Paquito weighed 120 kilos (265 pounds), lived to please his wife so that she would not leave him because of his weight, and took out increasingly larger loans to support the kitchen-sink business.

Fred, weighing 72 kilos (159 pounds), attended therapy to continue working on his fears, while his career continued to advance.

The two brothers were born identical, but grew up completely differently. One was a living example of what limiting beliefs generate, and the other, an example of empowering beliefs. For those who do not understand the mind, it seemed unbelievable that these twins were so different.

The last meeting of the brothers was when they met in the emergency room of a hospital, both infected with Covid-19. Paco ended up intubated for fifteen days, since his immune system had deteriorated due to hypertension and to the chronic inflammation that his overweight caused. Fred, asymptomatic, repeated the test in two weeks, with a negative result.

Health, money and love in our lives are not products of magic. They depend on whether we work on our limiting beliefs and turn them into empowering beliefs.

Answer the following questions to transform one of your limiting beliefs. Many times, if you ask someone you trust to help you do this exercise, the results can be even better.

1. What is the area of my life that I like the least today, that today generates a lot of anger, guilt, sadness or shame?

Example:
My financial situation. I barely survive on my present income and I often need to borrow money.

2. What actions brought me here? Make a list if necessary and answer honestly. Remember that, as an adult, only you are responsible for the results of your life. Don't judge yourself. The idea of the exercise is to take responsibility today and transform yourself.

Examples:
- When I received my pay, I didn't save any. I spent it all on outings or whims of the moment.

- I'm hate to get up early for English classes at 7 in the morning, despite the fact that this ability would help me to move up from my current job and find a better opportunity.

- I did not pay a debt on time and this prevented me from getting new credit to invest in a business.

3. What was this person thinking when he carried out these actions?

Examples:
- I didn't think about my future. I focused only on my happiness at the moment.

- I thought I would study English later and didn't foresee possibilities, such as that the pandemic would come and the opportunities could be reduced.

- I thought I knew how to manage my personal finances and didn't educate myself on how to handle a credit card before using it.

4. What limiting beliefs could be behind these actions? Brainstorm ideas, no matter how absurd they may seem. You might find it helpful to ask close friends or family what kind of beliefs they have in similar areas, since we tend to adopts the beliefs of the people we grew up with.

Examples:
- I'm not able to manage my personal finances.

- I don't deserve to have money.

- I'm unable to produce more money.

- I'm destined for poverty because everyone in my family has financial problems.

- Having money is dangerous because I might be robbed, as many people are. It's better not have money.

- The rich are bad. It's better to be poor but good.

- I prefer not to have money, but not to be alone. My family excludes those who are doing well.

- Having money is very difficult.

5. From the list above, choose one belief that you think has had the most impact on this aspect of your life.

6. Challenge this belief. Ask yourself enough questions to determine if this belief is true. Is it true that (write the belief from question 5)?

Example:
Do I have a physical, mental or emotional impediment that does not allow me to generate money? No. So, if I haven't been able to generate more money so far, it's not because it's impossible for me. If there is no impediment of any kind, what does generating more money today depend on? It depends on having the right knowledge and applying it. Have I looked for the right information on how to make more money? Have I tried hard enough to put this information into action? The truth is that, honestly, I have not. I have not sought the correct advice nor have I made any changes. So it is not true that I am unable to produce more money. If I educate myself and make an effort, I'll be able to generate more money.

7. What is the empowering belief behind the limiting belief?

Example:
My ability depends on my knowledge and my effort. I choose today to learn how to generate more money within my current circumstances and I choose to put effort into it.

8. List the proactive steps that can help you achieve the results you want, prioritize them and implement them one by one until you achieve the results you desire. If you do not achieve your desired results, it is because some other limiting beliefs are still active. In that case, do this exercise again.

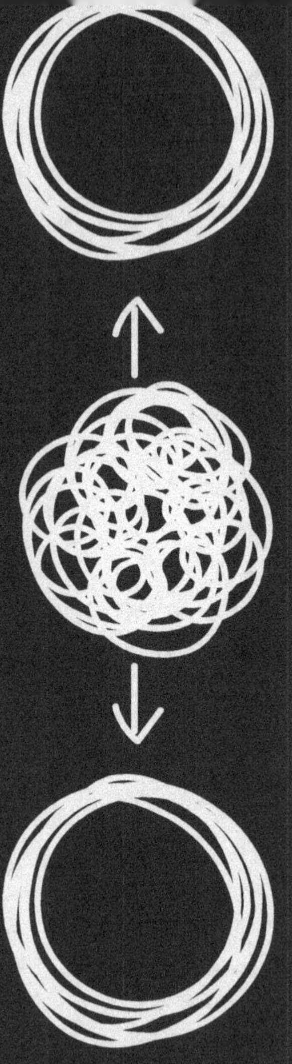

2

HOW CAN WE CHALLENGE
LIMITING BELIEFS?

The seeds of our results are beliefs. Beliefs are the reasons that we have or don't have money, health and love—in other words, *fulfillment*. Beliefs are also the basis for human survival.

Happiness is something changeable
that depends on whether we find
what we wanted. On the other hand,
fulfillment is an internal state that we
choose, in which we can be happy.

Whoever knows how to find beliefs that stop him or her and can change them, is the richest person on the planet because he or she has the destiny of his life in his hands. Those who cannot achieve this will always depend on happiness: "If people love me **today**, if I'm healthy and I have money, then I'm happy." But if something fails, everything collapses easily.

The great assistant

Our brain is like an executive assistant that speaks a thousand languages, is well trained, is super-efficient and does what we ask of it. But in the end the brain is just an assistant that has no power to decide on important matters. It needs direction; it needs a boss to teach it to think; to set a goal for it, to remove a **limiting** belief and install an **empowering** one.

Install and uninstall beliefs

There are three **simultaneous** tools to teach our great assistant to move from limiting beliefs to empowering ones. These tools imply a lifestyle in which constant practice is required.

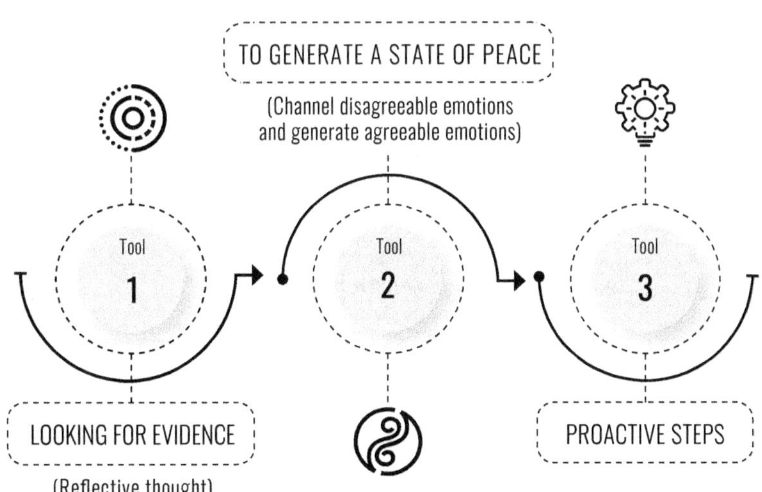

Tool 1: Looking for evidence

Reflective thought

There are many ways of thinking: creative, analytical, critical, systemic, etc. But only **reflective** thinking is needed to modify our beliefs.

Reflective thinking is learning to look
for the evidence behind our beliefs.

Let's remember that **limiting beliefs** are ideas that we take for granted without having evidence. Reflective thinking looks for those pieces of evidence. Reflective thinking pauses before adopting a hypothesis and turning it into a belief. The opposite of reflective thinking is self-deception: getting furious, looking for excuses and blaming others—in other words, saying things as absurd as, "I have not been successful in life because when I was born I had fetal distress."

Tool 2: Generating a state of peace

Channel unpleasant emotions and generate pleasant emotions

The search for evidence is a process that requires time. During that time, it is necessary to generate equanimity or a **state of peace** so that anxiety does not eat us up. Then we can look for evidence with relative tranquility.

Emotions are the fuel we need to
be able to search for evidence. And
that is why **Tool 1** and **Tool 2** must
be applied **simultaneously**.

If we do not have a **state of peace**, we run the risk of ending up with that gasoline of emotions necessary to search for evidence.

To achieve this tranquility we have to
learn to channel unpleasant emotions
and generate pleasant emotions.

Imagine that human beings have a bucket for our emotions. This container has a limit; we can't pretend that if we turn on a faucet to fill the bucket, it will never overflow. In the same way, we can't pretend that if we repeatedly feel fear or anger, these emotions will never exceed our bucket's capacity. The **state of peace** is like channeling that emotional water; it's like opening a safety valve in the bucket so that the water does not stagnate or overflow. Once we learn to release accumulated unpleasant emotions from the body, we can generate pleasant emotions.

Tool 3: Taking proactive steps

Grow or die

There are two ways of living: growing or dying, with no intermediate points.

If we are not growing in every aspect of our lives, we are dying. We know we are growing because we feel uncomfortable. At every moment, we have the opportunity to choose between one option or another.

Proactive steps don't have to do with
the moral concepts of "good" or "bad,"
but with being conscious, or not,
and accepting the consequences.

The opposite of proactive steps are reactive steps—in other words, actions carried out without thinking about the consequences or damage we can cause, and without thinking about whether an action is destructive or destructive.

For example, imagine saying, "I don't know when our relationship ended." But no relationship is destroyed by magic; the couple had thousands of opportunities to act, actively or reactively, every second. Or "I don't know when I got so fat." But gaining weight requires months of repeatedly choosing not to eat nutritious food. No one busts a pair of pants from a single slice of cake.

Reactivity will be reflected in unpleasant
effects; proactivity in pleasant effects.

To understand how these three tools work and why it's so important to transform our limiting beliefs, let's use an example:

- **Expected result:** To have a relationship based on love
- **Limiting belief:** They always leave me.

<table>
<tr><td colspan="3" align="center">TOOL</td></tr>
<tr><td align="center">1</td><td align="center">2</td><td align="center">3</td></tr>
<tr><td align="center">Look for evidence or think it over</td><td align="center">Generate a state of peace</td><td align="center">Take proactive and intelligent steps</td></tr>
</table>

EXPERIENCE — Applying the three tools

Look for evidence or think it over	Generate a state of peace	Take proactive and intelligent steps
The person observes that several relationships have failed and becomes aware that perhaps they were not just unfortunate coincidences. Perhaps the person himself, or herself, somehow, unintentionally, has caused a pattern. He or she wonders: "Am I the one generating this?" They become dedicated to looking for evidence: reading books, attending conferences, enrolling in a relationship course. When the person has more information about themselves, they look for an expert to help dig deeper, and become aware, for the first time, that an old wound of abandonment from childhood is still active, even after many years.	Meanwhile, as the person is managing to identify and dismantle the limiting beliefs that prevent the relationship they long for from being built, they carry out a daily routine suggested by a coach, in which they spend time writing how they feel and what they've been learning. During this process, they go for walks or do body stretches to energize themselves for each new day. On days when they feel very anxious that they are going to be abandoned again, they call a friend so that they feel accompanied and heard.	The person gives themselves the opportunity to meet different candidates while remaining aware of their fear of being abandoned and their genuine desire to love and be loved. Slowly, they look at themselves and the other person. When they discover that the other person is also working on themselves, this gives them the opportunity to be vulnerable, to open their heart. Instead of self-sabotaging, when the person feels anxious and sorry for themselves, they understand that they are in a process of challenging their own limiting beliefs, that there is no rush, and that nothing and no one can abandon or hurt them unless they themselves do so or allow it to happen.

 1 **NOT looking for evidence or thinking it over**	 2 **NOT generating a state of peace**	 3 **NOT taking proactive and intelligent steps**
The person isn't aware that abandonment is caused by their limiting belief and not because that's how the world is. They are completely convinced that the people they have relationships with will always abandon them, although there are many other possible outcomes.	The person knows different candidates with whom to enter into the relationship they long for. Even though these candidates do nothing to suggest that they're going to leave, the person constantly feels anxious, creating catastrophic hypotheses that pain them. These could be, "I'm sure that they promised me they won't leave me in order to manipulate me." "If I'm careless, they'll leave me faster." "I'm sure they are thinking about another person."	In order to escape or stop the enormous doses of anxiety produced by "the expected abandonment," the person self-sabotages and unconsciously sabotages the potential relationship. Some examples of reactive actions of sabotage are: being unfaithful, constantly rejecting or minimizing the other person, demanding excessive attention or choosing, from all the candidates, the most dangerous person, so that there won't be any other option but to leave them.

The left edge of the table above is labelled vertically: **EXPERIENCE** — **NOT** applying the three tools

RESULTS OBTAINED

The left edge of the section below is labelled vertically: **EXPERIENCE**

Applying the three tools	The anxiety about abandonment decreases considerably, or at least, little by little, becomes more and more successfully channeled. The person realizes that the only person who can abandon one is oneself, because if someone else does abandon one, the effect, if one has oneself, will always be growth and fulfillment.
NOT applying the three tools	Abandonment, above all abandonment of oneself. The person, instead of understanding that it was he or she who created the situation and who abandoned the possible relationship, or sabotaged it, confirms that the limiting belief is true: "You see, everyone leaves me." Anxiety increases.

Life is full of accidents: Covid, the world economy, toxic people and a long etcetera. However, we can interpret all catastrophes as pretexts.

The arrival of a catastrophe is not as important as being trained in how to receive it. If we haven't prepared ourselves with reflective thinking, channeled emotions, and taking proactive steps, how can we expect to survive a crisis?

To try to win a marathon without prior training is a great example of craziness.

Double life

January 2008. Monterrey, Mexico

Laura joins a gym and plans to run a marathon in Belgium. She thinks that's a good option to get away from her routine for a few days, since a triangle drawn by her children, her husband and her job had brought her chronic migraines.

April 2008. Monterrey, Mexico

Laura meets Emilio at the gym reception. They start dating after workouts. Both explain to their spouses that their exercise routines have become more extensive and that is why they take longer to get home. They go to places different from their normal routines to avoid being seen by someone they know.

April 2010. Vallarta triathlon

They share the same room and the same experiences: adrenaline rushes, limiting beliefs, sentimental catastrophes and seeking to generate pleasant emotions to cover the problems they have at home.

January 2010. Monterrey

Laura's husband is suspicious and hires a private detective. He has also been looking for evidence in their relationship, which has been broken by the years. He finds evidence. Desperate, he threatens to kill Emilio. Far from employing any reflective thought, Laura's husband has decided to deceive himself, thinking that this is the solution.

September 2011. Bruges, Belgium

Laura, looking for tranquility and a state of peace, assumes the consequences and decides to end her marriage. With two children and in search of empowering beliefs, she moves to another country

February, 2013. Atlanta, Georgia

Emilio and Laura get married. They continue searching for the state of peace and tranquility that they have still not found, despite the fact that they have tried to modify the world around them.

Although some would consider this story to have a good *ending*, since Laura finally ended up married and in peace, the reality is that she achieved the result she hoped for (a functional relationship) by the long route—the route of suffering. One possible shorter path, with less burden of pain, could have started in January 2008, when her chronic migraines perhaps announced that she was not entirely *happy* with her life. She could have stopped to reflect on what changes she needed to feel fulfilled and taken note of the matter. She might have realized at that point that her marriage was no longer *alive*, and she could have avoided the painful experience of infidelity—and ended the cycle *in* a *healthy* way. Probably Emilio himself would have appeared some time later, and would have been spared the guilt and shame that two years of living a double life generated.

> Fulfillment comes when we have
> the courage to face and accept the
> fact that we are not happy with our
> achievements and to change our inner
> state to achieve what we want.

Think of a person you admire a lot. If you are close to the person, interview them and ask how they managed to be or do what you admire. Ask them about obstacles and how they overcame the obstacles. Write down any empowering beliefs, or ways they created peaceful states (or how they channeled their emotions), and any proactive steps they took.

If the person is not close to you, look for interviews, videos and documentaries about their life and try to answer the same three questions.

Person you admire:

What did they do to achieve being or doing what you admire?

Have they had obstacles?

How did they overcome them?

Empowering beliefs:

Peaceful states:

Proactive steps:

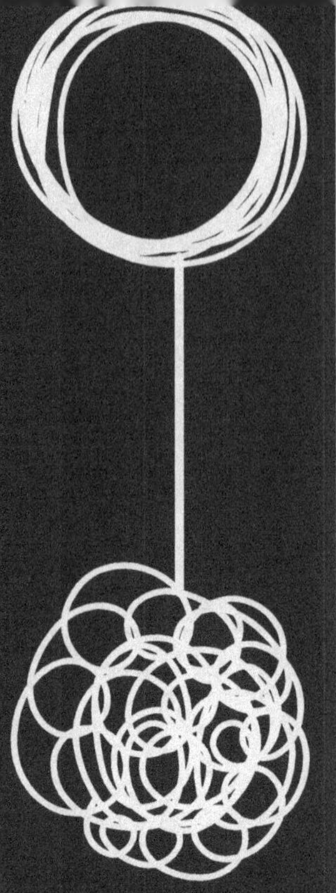

3

WHAT IS REFLECTIVE
THOUGHT?

Reflective thinking is the **careful**, **continual**, persistence of accepting beliefs based only on evidence. If there is no evidence we should not accept an idea, although it is worth putting the idea on pause until proof is found.

The objective of reflective thinking

The objective or purpose is to create meaning, that is, to experience any situation, from the very insignificant to the most complex, and find the meaning in a situation or simply let it pass us by. Both are valid.

If we find, seek or build the meaning of things that happen to us, what happens is that we learn from the event and from ourselves. And, therefore, we grow. If we just let things go by without making sense of them, then we are destined to always make the same mistake and get stuck.

By finding meaning, we learn from
experiences so that, if they were
destructive, they do not repeat
themselves. Or, if they were constructive,
we create more such experiences.

Finding meaning generates learning and leads to growth, which makes it easier for all our energy to focus on evolving and not on repeating patterns, like a hamster running on its wheel without going anywhere.

Reflective thought and finding
meaning are matters of survival.

Logotherapy

This search is the foundation of logotherapy, in which Victor Flankl proposes that finding *meaning* is the main motivation of human beings. He postulated, after observing people who survived in a concentration camp (where he was imprisoned for several years), that the fittest people were not the physically strongest, but rather those who had a meaning, a "why" or "*what for.*"

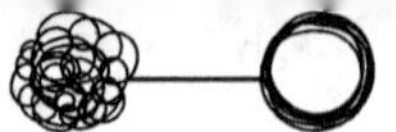

The "*what for*" of the meaning

In life, in every circumstance, we all go from an **initial state** to a **final state**, for example, from being overweight to having an ideal weight, from being single to finding a good partner, from poverty to abundance; that is, from emptiness to fullness.

The **initial state** is everything we are used to (be it a toxic or constructive situation). Generally, it is *normal* to experience the initial state with **little awareness** of it, and it usually involves **habitual actions**. In this state there is an **apparent balance**, because we are static; we do not move; we are fixed in that particular circumstance.

When leaving the **initial state** we always go through **imbalance**. We cannot reach a final goal if we do not submit to a necessary state of **chaos**, because the **final state** is *different* from the **initial state**, and any change implies abandoning comfort in order to achieve improvement.

We can't get something new if
we don't deconstruct the old.

If we set sail on a ship, we may necessarily have to go through a storm to reach the next port. The important thing is not to lose our compass and to know where we are going, even if the waves buffet us and the wind blows. The port from which we leave is the **initial state**. The storm is the necessary **imbalance**, a part of the process, a part of the natural law involved in reaching the **final destination (the new port)**. The important thing is not to lose the compass. What is dangerous is not the storm, but forgetting the meaning, or "why" we are going through this process.

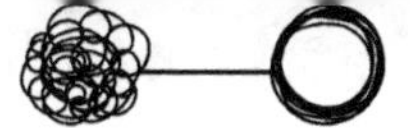

A new empowering belief is: It doesn't
matter if a storm of imbalance hits me.
As long as I don't lose the compass
of meaning, I can reach the goal.

The **final state** is your goal—the *future experience* that you reach with *greater awareness*, filled with a new **balance** thanks to *action that is intelligent* and disruptive.

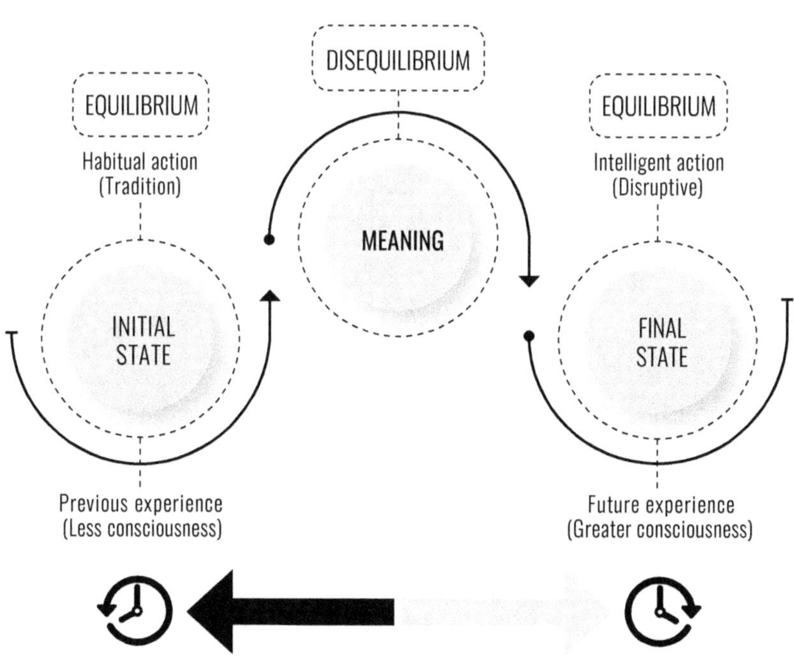

Some questions to find the meaning of what happens to us could be: If this experience had a "why" or "for what," what would it be? What things can I learn from this experience that I didn't know before?

The answer to "why" can come from the circumstance itself, or we can figure it out.

The **final state** is something that we want very much. But it may happen that when we think about the "why," we don't find any meaning. In that case, it is worthwhile to rethink or reframe the goal.

For example, perhaps we believe that our ultimate goal is to have a million dollars. When finally, after much work, we get the money and buy a car for a thousand dollars, then we no longer have a million dollars, but a million minus a thousand. In this case, was having that million really the final state? Considering the "why" or "what for" could lead us to discover that the final state was not really that amount of money, but to feel successful in business.

> On our journey, we realize that the
> ultimate goal, generally, was not material,
> but was connected with **_fulfillment_**.

If the final state is an experience in the future, then where does that leave the here and now?

While we may have goals that will occur over time, living with an eye on the future will not help the goal materialize faster. On the contrary, it only provokes anxiety. It doesn't help to turn constantly to the past to try to justify our failures either. This only brings us depression. The here and now is the only place not only to initiate or keep on the path toward a goal, but it is the only place where we can feel fulfillment and peace. The here and now is the only place that exists.

Depression is an excess of the past; anxiety is an excess of the future.

To live in the present is to be in peace.

Dalai Lama.

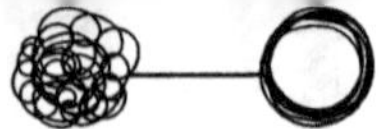

Conditions for reflective thought

There are three basic conditions for reflective thinking to occur: it needs to occur in community, it needs to be systematic and rigorous, and it should be based on a need for growth and contribution to the world.

Community

This means engaging with someone else to generate reflective thinking. This can mean anything from reading a book or watching a movie to interacting with those who created them, to talking with another person, taking a course or a workshop, watching a Ted *Talk*, looking for a coach, etc.—in other words, being open to the world.

If we are isolated it is more complicated to answer our "why" and "*what for*" questions. Isolated, we might end up with superficial answers that are subject to our personal distortions and paradigms.

> Doing reflective thinking in community takes us out of our *interior* or inner reality.

A rigorous system

We can find the "why" and "what for" of our situation through reflective thinking, but if, over time, we do not continue to question ourselves about the matter, we may no longer be exercising reflective thinking, but instead forging beliefs.

We need to insist, keep questioning, and be **rigorous** and **systematic**. This is where the definition of reflective thinking that we talked about at the beginning of this chapter comes from: "Reflective thinking is the careful, **continual**, **persistence** of accepting beliefs based only on evidence."

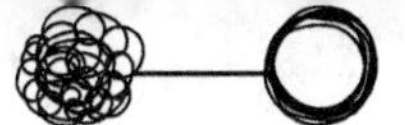

We shouldn't ask "why" and "what
for" only at the New Year, our birthday,
or even every time we get drunk.

Growth and contribution

Reflective thinking is based on an authentic need to **grow** and **contribute** to the world, which we will look at in detail just ahead.

Reflective thinking step by step

How do we achieve a **continual**, **careful** persistence in accepting beliefs only if we have evidence?

Step 1

Step 1 is the experience itself that we are living in—for example, the Covid-19 pandemic.

Step 2

Step 2 is the spontaneous interpretation of an experience, the initial, emotional and careless reaction that we have. In the example of Covid-19 this could be: "I'm going to get infected, die or lose my job. I can't handle the home office option," and so on. This is as far as most people get.

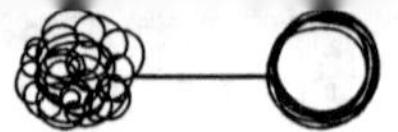

Step 3

Step 3 consists of naming problem or questions that arise from an experience, and verbalizing them. In the case of Covid-19:

a) My health is at risk.

b) I could lose my job and have a financial crisis.

c) To survive I may need to do something different, learn a new trade from scratch, and so on.

Step 4

Step 4 is to imagine possible solutions to the problems you identified in Step 3.

a) Research how to take care of myself during the pandemic.

b) Learn to generate a parallel source of income, such as passive income.

c) Research what trades or abilities are necessary today and take a night course online.

Step 5

Transform the possible solutions into hypotheses:

a) Is it true that if I exercise, eat well and take similar measures, my health can be protected?

b) Is it true that if I find a way to generate passive income, I can recover financially?

c) Is it true that if every night, Monday to Friday, I take tutorials in a new, virtual skill, I can adapt better?

Step 6

Look for evidence of these hypotheses, that is, try some of them out to see if they really work:

a) Start a balanced diet, exercise, faithfully wash the hands, maintain a healthy distance from others and use a mask.

b) Research ways to generate passive income and try one of them.

c) Watch a tutorial every night to learn a new skill.

Step 7

If any action doesn't have good results, go back to Step 4 and repeat the process until you are moving towards your goals.

> **Nota:** There are times in which the first hypothesis helps us overcome problems. Other situations require many hypotheses and tests. Don't be quick to judge yourself harshly or stop moving. The most successful people in the world often put a thousand hypotheses into action. Remember that the most dangerous thing isn't the storm, but losing your compass.

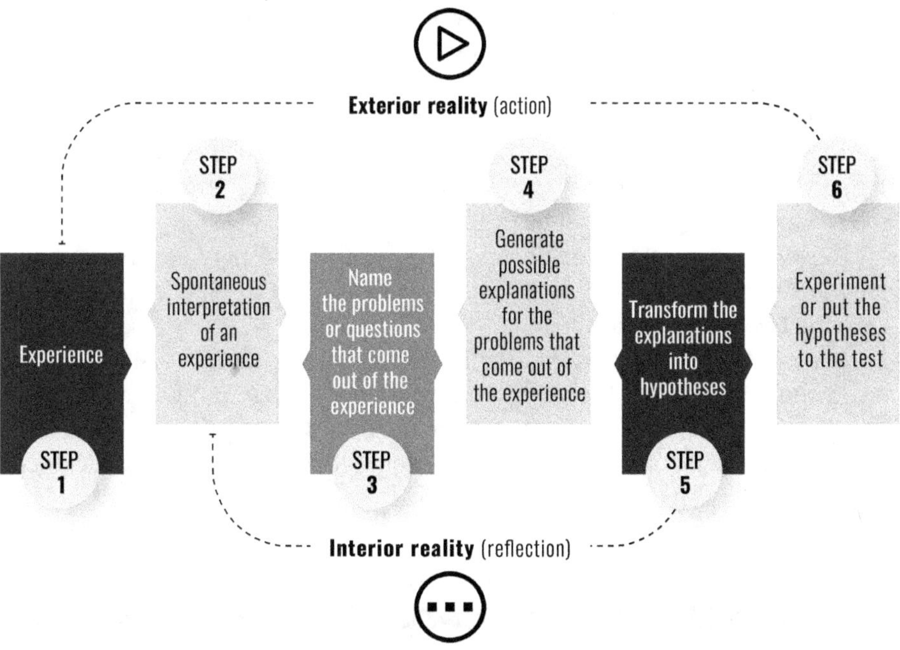

Silence doesn't cure cancer

Margara began with intense pain in the pit of her stomach, accelerated hair loss, and sudden dizziness. Blanca, her eldest daughter, with whom she lived, was a nurse at a general hospital, and had seen this situation several times in cancer patients. So she asked her friend, Dr. Casales, to run tests on Margara, praying that her suspicion was wrong. A few weeks later, in an emotional call, the doctor said Márgara had stage-four cancer of the esophagus.

Margara had an unpleasant family situation. She had three daughters and two sons, and, with the exception of Blanca, all of them had distanced themselves from her because of her bitterness and aggressiveness. Her excuse was her childhood years in the middle of a war and the loss of her parents at the age of 9. With the symptoms of the last few months, she knew that perhaps the end was near, and her fear of dying had increased the complaints of life and her emotional blackmailing of Blanca.

Despite the fact that for decades the relationship between mother and daughter had been toxic and Margara had interfered in Blanca's every decision, the two had a visible codependency.

Blanca called her brothers to tell them about her mother's situation and asked them not to tell her anything, to let her die ignorant, but in peace, thinking of the saying, "Eyes that do not see, heart that does not feel." Her hypothesis was that maybe if her mother found out she had advanced cancer, she would die even faster.

The younger sister, Alicia, despite the fact that she had not seen her mother in two years, did not agree with Blanca. She had just read in a women's magazine that "if they discover the meaning of the things that happen to them, they will be victorious in anything." This seemed like a sign from heaven. Alicia told her brothers and sisters that if they hid the cancer from their mother, Margara would miss out, not only on finding the meaning of the disease, but also on her last chance to change and vindicate all the damage she had done.

Margara died two and a half years after that discussion between the siblings. How did she cope with her illness in the last 18 months? Did she go on a retreat and recover her relationship with her family? Did she go on vacation to her home country and finally feel free and fulfilled? Did she start a nutrition and yoga program to try to cure herself? Did she write a book of repentance so that everyone with cancer could say goodbye with dignity? Or, as Blanca predicted, did he hasten her death?

None of the above occurred. The reason was that Margara never knew what she really had. Neither Blanca, nor Alicia nor the other three children said anything, and Margara did not want to investigate why her condition kept deteriorating, as if silence could cure cancer. She died scared, alone with her daughter Blanca, who was codependent and full of guilt because she hadn't even started the reflective thought process of accepting the experience. As the article Alicia read said:

"No matter how serious what is happening may be, if you make sense out of it, thousands of possibilities will always open up. But if you don't even dare to accept the experience, there is simply nothing that can be done."

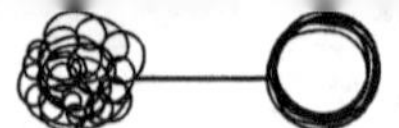

Five 'why' and 'what for' **exercises**

To find the meaning of the things you do, of a relationship or of your own life, an excellent exercise is to answer the question "**What for?**" five times. Choose a topic whose meaning you want to discover and start by asking yourself why you do, or support, that aspect of your life. To your answers, again "What for?" and so on until you have completed the five repetitions. Look at the following example:

Theme to reflect upon:	Money

"What for?" 1	**What do I want money for?**
	To be able to cover basic necessities (home, clothes, food) and to be able to have luxuries (travel, education, parties)
"What for?" 2	**Why do I want to be able to cover my basic necessities and luxuries?**
	I want to cover my basic necessities to survive and luxuries to have fun.
"What for?" 3	**What do I want to survive and have fun for?**
	I want to survive to be able to carry out my mission in life. I want to have fun so that my life isn't just slavery but instead I can feel free.
"What for?" 4	**Why do I want to carry out my mission in life and feel free?**
	I want to carry out my life's mission so that I can help a lot of people, and I want to feel free in order to feel alive.
"What for?" 5	**Why do I want to help many people and feel alive?**
	I want to help a lot of people so that they can live in love and not suffering, and I want to feel alive to take advantage of and enjoy life.

Conclusion: *For me the meaning of money is that it is a vehicle to accompany people living their life in love and a vehicle to remember that life is a gift and it is important to take advantage of and enjoy life. This is very different from trying to earn money every day because of an obsession with money itself. This exercise has given money a new meaning for me as a means to live in love and fulfillment.*

When you find ultimate meaning behind what you do and choose, your life, your perspective, and your motivation are transformed. Don't hesitate to apply this exercise to all the important aspects of your life and to all matters in which you need to make the best decision.

4

TRANSFORM
YOUR EMOTIONS

An emotion is energy in movement. It occurs in your body and is physical energy—more specifically, electromagnetic and biochemical energy. For this reason, emotional energy can be measured in both its electromagnetic and biochemical forms.

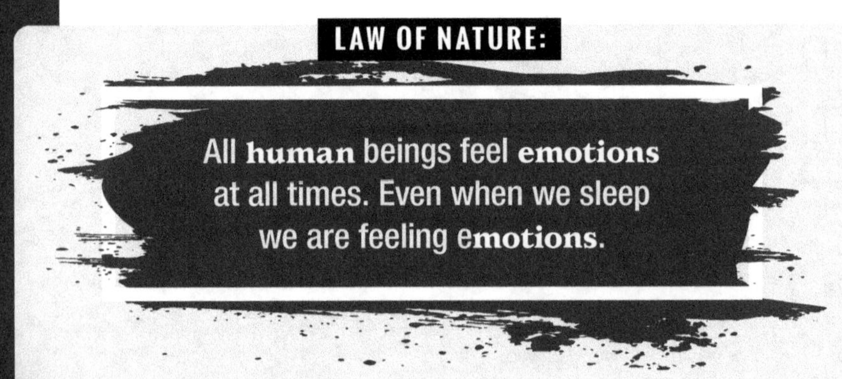

The brain never stops, so neither do the emotions. When someone says they don't feel anything, it's simply because at that moment he or she doesn't have a conscious connection with their body or emotions.

Emotions are not optional.
Feelings are inescapable.

Emotional **GPS**

There are only two types of emotions: **agreeable** and **disagreeable**. Emotions are not classified as *good* or *bad*—they are messages that are answers to the question:

"Faced with this situation, what
should I do, or what type of
person should I become, in order
to feel fulfilled and to grow?"

Many people believe that emotions are a bother, that we would be better off without them. In the world there is tremendous social confusion that having feelings is bad. If you are crying, you are told "Don't cry." If angry, "Don't be angry." If you feel love, "Don't get stuck; don't exaggerate," and so on. But nature is never wrong.

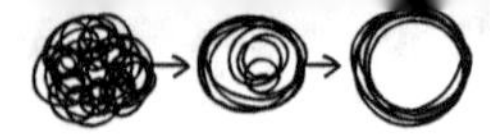

Emotions are the GPS of your life.
If we didn't have this emotional
apparatus, we would get lost.

When we set ourselves a goal of health, money or love, we tell our GPS where we are going. Our emotional apparatus guides us to get closer to our destination. If we are on the right track, we know it thanks to **pleasant** emotions. If by mistake we take a route that takes us away from our goal, our GPS will tell us through **unpleasant** emotions.

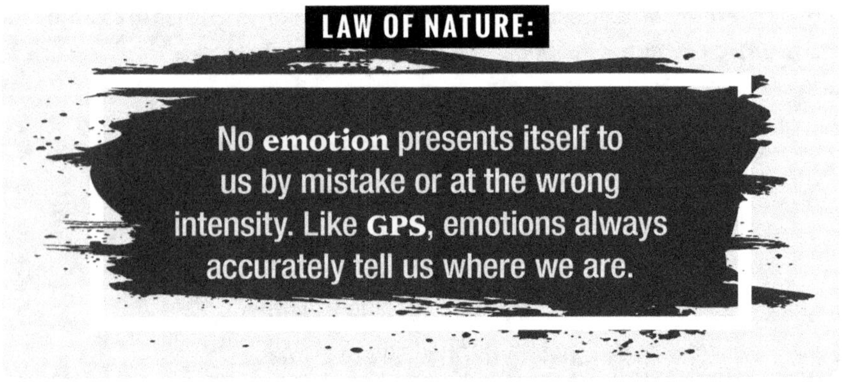

With each turn in the road, GPS tells us if we are on the right track or not. In the same way, each emotion, pleasant or unpleasant, tells us if our belief will help us achieve our goal or not. The emotional response of each person depends on their own project of fulfillment.

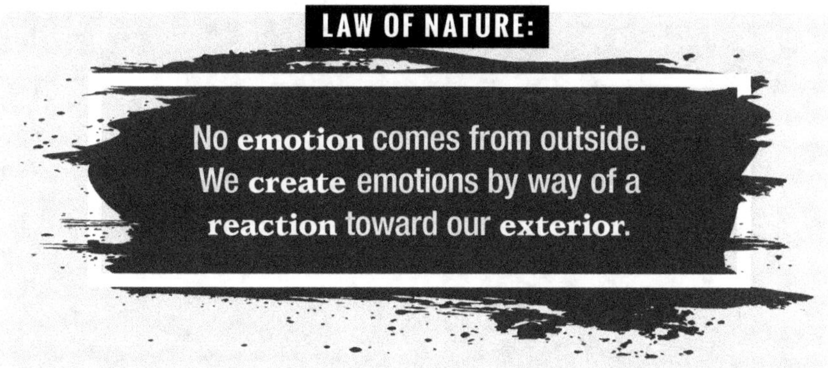

To redirect the route of our emotions, what we must generally change is our belief system. No emotion comes without a preceding thought and there is no thought without an underlying belief.

Every time we experience an emotion, it is because we need to hear a message to reach fulfillment, and that message guides us to know what we should do and into whom we should build ourselves.

In moments of crisis, when circumstances overwhelm us, it is difficult to see that emotions are not coming from outside. But emotions do not come from things, people or crises. Emotions are not entities that enter our head like a cloud.

Emotions are the product of the alignment or misalignment of our beliefs with the events that are presented to us.

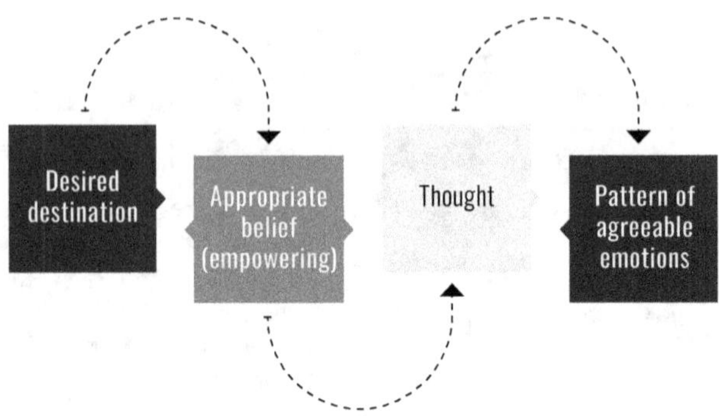

The function of emotions

Emotions can be classified in many ways. We will use one the way that has a very easy-to-remember mnemonic—FALSH—organizing the types of emotions by their first letter.

GROUP	FUNCTION	ENERGY LEVEL
Fear	To survive; be alert to threats	High or very high
Anger	To place limits; more than anything, limits on ourselves	High or very high
Love	Connection; to express what we love	High or very high
Sadness	To reflect; to pause	Low or very low
Happiness	To celebrate	High or very high

Fear

Our emotional apparatus developed in the first human beings to allow them to survive, but it is not well adapted to the times we live in today.

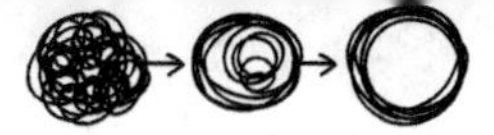

This emotional apparatus made *homo* sapiens feel fear in order to generate enough adrenaline so that their arms and legs were ready to fight or to flee in the face of a real threat: a wild animal, a landslide, etc.

Even though we now live in a technological civilization surrounded and we don't experience the same kind of dangers; we still have practically the same emotional apparatus.

Today, 99.9% of the threats we feel
are unreal. Although giving a speech in
public does not put our lives at risk, it
still activates an alert level equivalent to
when we are about to be eaten by a tiger.

Today, we don't find saber-toothed tigers on the corner. Instead we fear things like facing a boss, a podium on a stage, a disappointment in love or an expired credit card—situations that do not directly and immediately threaten our physical integrity.

Today, when fear appears, nobody reminds us that we are no longer that primitive man of thousands of years ago who was afraid because his life was at serious risk. Today, the worst that can happen is the boss denies us a raise when we ask for it. The vast majority of the time, we will not die if he or she says no.

Fear can come in different intensities, from "I'm nervous" or feeling anxious, to panic attacks or anxiety disorders.

In the face of fear, what should I do?
What kind of person should I build myself
into so that I can grow and be fulfilled?

The initial response should be to check whether our survival or our physical integrity are truly at risk. If they are not at risk, as is the case most of the time, then our response should be to face and live what frightens us. In other words, the invitation of fear is to be brave.

All human beings who do not have a psychosis or mental illness feel fear—**all** of us. Today, the most common fears come from not being loved and from not belonging.

Joy and love

Joy and love are also necessary for survival. Love has to do with connecting with our tribe (our family and friends), and joy with expressing and celebrating the fact that we are moving forward on the path to wholeness.

> In the face of joy and love, what
> should I do? In whom should I build
> myself to grow and be in fullness?

We need to thank and appreciate that we have a tribe, be it family, friends, work team, country or world. We also need to appreciate, be thankful and celebrate that we are alive and that one way to honor the gift of life is to connect with others, allowing ourselves to touch and be touched in our hearts.

> Joy and love confirm that we are allowing
> ourselves to be loved and to belong.

Sadness

Remember that emotions are energy in motion in our body and sadness is one of the emotions that has less energy. The other groups of emotions are of high energy, because with them we need to act. On the other hand, sadness is low energy because it tells us to stop—to stop a little to reflect, to pause.

We generally feel sad in the face of a loss, and this emotion helps us to meditate on what we no longer have, whether it is something material or not.

In the face of sadness, what should I
do, into whom should I build myself
in order to grow and be fulfilled?

What we need is to reflect on what we lost, to let go, let go, to reimagine the meaning of our life without the other person, to embrace the pain and to forgive.

Many people make the mistake of reacting to sadness by ignoring or covering it up with alcohol or other substances, causing a disaster.

Anger

The function of anger is to set limits; that's why it has high energy. Beware. Most people believe that these limits must be placed outside, in the outside world, and that is why they shout and hit. No. That reaction involves low emotional intelligence. Instead, we must often place the limits inward, towards ourselves in our inner world.

In the face of anger, what should I
do, into whom should I build myself
in order to grow and be fulfilled?

We need to identify what any behavior that we have been practicing in an excessive manner is, and put a limit on it.

In general, the three steps to follow when we feel any unpleasant emotion are:

STEP 1

Acknowledge the emotion, either while feeling it or later. Ideally, recognize an emotion at the moment and stop any action we're engaged in.

STEP 2

Channel it; using emotional intelligence techniques, remove the energy and hormones produced by the emotion from the body.

STEP 3

Listen to the message. With a *cool head* now, listen to the message of the emotion—whether it is to be brave and throw myself into what scares me; or in the case of sadness to accept and pardon; or in the case of anger, to put the brakes on what I'm doing, even for several weeks.

STEP 4

Execute as soon as possible the action that the emotion indicates to me.

Emotional energy

As energy, emotions obey the first law of thermodynamics: "Energy cannot be created or destroyed; it can only be transformed."

When we are presented with an emotion, we cannot simply cancel it. A transformation is required. Usually people advise someone else to repress, avoid or suppress emotions to try to get rid of them. What these bad practices achieve is that emotions intensify and accumulate, leading to more conflict or illness. A person may hear advice such as "Go out with your friends to a party. That way you'll forget you broke up with your boyfriend"—as if by magic, being distracted or not looking at the emotion will make it disappear!

> An emotion does not disappear just like that, with evasive techniques. In fact, the opposite happens. Emotions can only be transformed if they is made conscious and acted upon.

But the physical energy remains, accumulating, and even somatizing—impacting body cells due to an excess of hormones. We must learn to transform emotions.

American psychiatrist David Ramon Hawkins studied the energy of emotions and proposed the following scheme in which he measures their energy in hertz (Hz), which are units to quantify the frequency of electromagnetic waves.

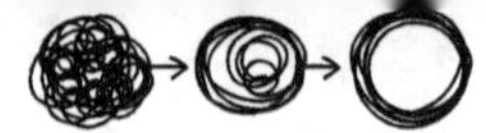

HEALTH SICKNESS

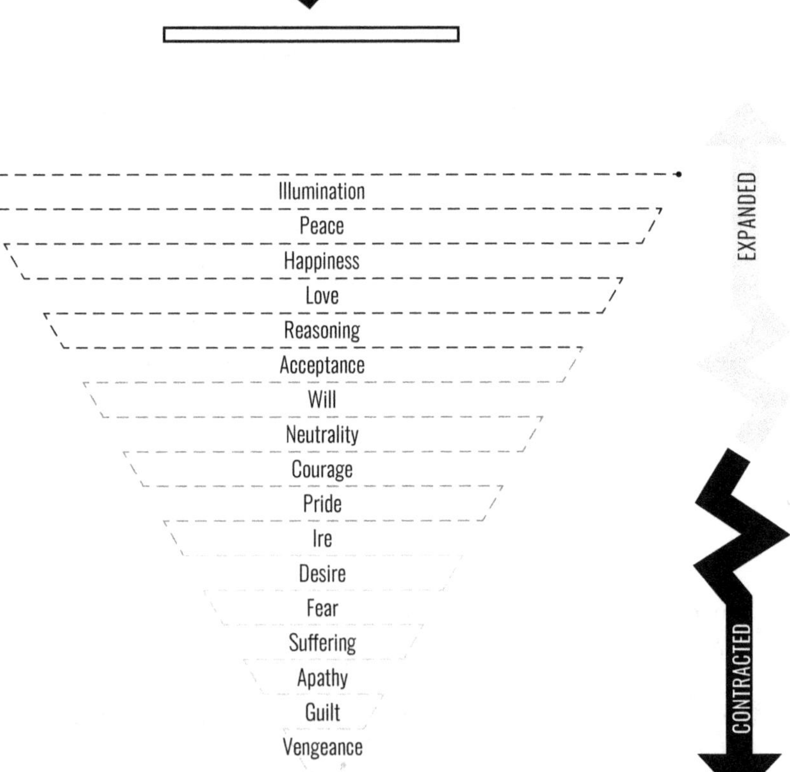

HEALTH
SICKNESS
EXPANDED
CONTRACTED
Illumination
Peace
Happiness
Love
Reasoning
Acceptance
Will
Neutrality
Courage
Pride
Ire
Desire
Fear
Suffering
Apathy
Guilt
Vengeance

As we already mentioned, when we give our emotional GPS a destination, it indicates the route, and if we deviate it launches unpleasant alerts. If we ignore those alarms, the GPS sends us stronger alerts and, if we ignore them, even noisier ones will launch. Then the moment comes when those alarms become a real nuisance; that is anxiety, and it comes with the intensity necessary for us to listen.

> Anxiety is accumulated fear from spending a lot of time without reflective thought, from living life without a why.

Anxiety belongs to the fear family. A person has many opportunities to listen to his GPS—it does not reach the point of anxiety or a panic attack overnight. Fear knocks on our door many times, first as a small messenger, until it becomes someone who has to kick down the door to deliver his message. Once again, since we are talking about survival, the fear will grow until the wisdom behind it is heard.

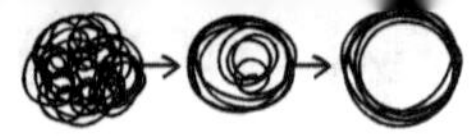

An **emotion** is always present
in the exact amount at the **exact**
moment so that we can **transform**
ourselves and be whole.

Although we may believe that anxiety
can sometimes feel disproportionate and
irrational, it complies with a natural law.

If we don't listen to fear, anxiety will arise, and if we don't listen to anxiety either, an anxiety disorder will arise.

Anxiety **disorder is an emotional** pattern in which the body is trapped in a vicious circle: anxiety triggers more hormones and these hormones trigger more anxiety, until you reach the feeling of losing total control of the body and mind.

Mexico City, Chilpancingo Metrobus station. 4:00 p.m.

Between the La Paz Viaduct station and Chilpancingo a Metrobus is traveling along the large avenue Baja California. Two cyclists are unable to cross and get in the bike lane. The bus slows down, tries to get out of the lane so as not to hit them, succeeds, but then collides with a power pole.

"Dear God!" shouted a lady on the bus who had hit a handrail. The woman was on her way to the hospital to visit her granddaughter, who had been in an incubator for six months. Her daughter, still a teenager, had suffered complications during her pregnancy.

The first thing she thought when she hit the rail was that she would not arrive in time for visiting hours. Her pain turned into suffering: she cried, she complained, she felt faint, and a drama began that further alarmed the other passengers.

"Keep calm, please," the driver asked in the midst of the confusion over having run over one of the cyclists. After a year and a half without a job, this man had been working for the Mexico City Metrobus for a month. If it was proven that he was at fault, in a few days he could be unemployed and even arrested. Faced with this threat, he thinks about running away. His fear is so strong that his stomach turns over.

"Is anyone injured?" asks a young college graduate who had been looking for an online consulting provider for construction companies. At the time of the accident, he helped an elderly couple to get up, picked up two cell phones from the floor and handed them to their owners, called an ambulance, and opened the emergency exit on the roof. While the others were trembling or paralyzed with fright, this young man was full of life, with lucid and loving reactions towards his fellow accident victims. As his father always told him: "Just do good and don't think about who you are helping."

"Call an ambulance, I can't move my neck," said someone in the women's car. It was a lady sitting in the disabled area. Minutes before the accident, she had pretended to be asleep when a woman with a baby in her arms was looking for a place to sit. She is living in her own reality, within her own irresponsible existence. Now she doesn't act, is uninterested in others, and instead thinking this is a good opportunity for an accident that will allow her to get disability in the restaurant where she works. She insults the driver, the ambulance personnel and whoever is standing near her. While she does so, it is evident that she can move her neck. Her anger has invaded her.

"The police have arrived. This is going to be good," a man says as he smiles, takes out his cell phone and begins taking photos. Through the window he yells at an officer: "Commander, I saw everything. Several people were run over. It was because the driver was on the phone and not watching. Over there are several wounded people." Next he thought that now was a good time to sue the Secretary of Transportation for possible negligence. His desire and greed invade him, as he thinks it is an excellent opportunity to get money and continue a lazy life.

The same situation triggers radically different reactions in each person, ranging from apathy and fear to love and service. What do these very different reactions depend on? The emotional state we are in. It is not what happens to us, but what we do with it.

Techniques to channel emotions

There are many techniques to channel emotions. Here are some of the most efficient. They're focused on particular emotions and must be done systematically. Don't forget to scan the QR codes to learn in detail how they are done.

Reptile

This exercise consists of performing six breaths in a very particular way and with a special posture. Breaths should be deep, inhaling through the nose and exhaling through the mouth. In the last three, we inhale through the mouth, but when exhaling, we do it with a shout. These shouts should come from the abdomen so as not to hurt the vocal cords.

- **Helpful emotions**: fear

- **Frequency:** in crisis situations it is suggested to do them daily or as many times as necessary. If there is no crisis, once a week.

- Check the following video to see the correct form.

Writing

This consists of writing on a sheet of paper, openly and freely, without pausing, what happened in specific situations. It is valid to make harsh judgments and use bad language. Sometimes the wording may not even make sense. After finishing, write the word "Transmuted" over the text. Then tear up the paper and burn the pieces, or dispose of them so that nobody can read the contents.

- **Emotions in which this technique helps**: anger especially, although it also works for sadness and fear.

- **Frequency**: each time an event occurs. If there isn't an event, every day before bed.

- Check the following video to see the correct form:

Container

This consists of talking to another person about what hurts us, but in a very special dialogue—without receiving judgments or advice. This is why the characteristics of the interlocutor must be special:

- Interlocutor must know how to listen.

- Must keep things confidential.

- Interlocutor should not stay with his/her emotions.

- Should not give advice. However, can ask questions.

- **Helpful emotions**: sadness and fear

- **Frequency**: once a week. If there is a crisis, every day

Guided visualization

This is a neuro-linguistic programming technique using a specific meditation in which we visualize removing an unpleasant emotion from our system and replacing it with a pleasant one of greater power.

- **Emotions it helps with**: anger, sadness and fear

- **Frequency**: once a week or every day, if there is a crisis

Meditation

This is the art of being in the here and now, lasting at least 15 minutes. Remember that meditating has its difficulties, so it may be hard to discipline the mind and body for the first few weeks. Later it will become easier and much more pleasant. It is normal for the mind to go away, for us to fall asleep, etc. With further training, we can add more time to meditation.

- **Emotions it helps with**: any unpleasant emotions

- **Frequency**: every day.

Exercise

Exercise as a channeling technique must have certain characteristics: it must be challenging for our body, yet we must be cautious about our limitations. It is carried out with the intention of releasing or transmuting emotions that no longer serve us, and preferably alone. If we choose to listen to music, it should help us stay focused on the present and not distract us.

- **Helpful emotions**: anger and fear, with or without a crisis

- **Frequency**: every day

Contact with nature

This consists of putting our skin into contact with nature: smelling flowers, hugging trees (even a tree on the sidewalk), walking barefoot on the grass, etc.

- **Emotions in which it helps**: sadness

- **Frequency**: whenever possible

Nota: the secret of all these techniques is systematization, not only when there is a crisis. They must be a habit, only in this way will a correct emotional hygiene be obtained. Let's take care of our expectations when thinkingthat by doing them once we are already cured. Everything is a process.

Emotional diary

Using these0 diaries successfully potentiates the effect of the previous techniques, increases emotional intelligence and helps us to know ourselves better.

Emotional diary 1

Count how many times you felt these emotions and record the days on which you experienced them.

	M	T	W	Th	F	Sa	Su
Fear							
Happiness							
Sadness							
Anger							
Love							

Emotional diary 2

Register your emotions in detail.

Theme to	Theme		Theme
Brief description of the situation			Strategy I used to channel the emotion
Initial degree of emotion			Final degree of emotion

What did I learn?

5

PROACTIVE
ACTION

We cannot buy motivation in a store. If we are not motivated, we don't transform what we have learned into action. As we have already seen, in life there are two options: grow or die. Having no motivation is practically synonymous with dying.

Life happens in action.

We can be very good at reflective thought and have peaceful emotions, but if we do not act, a change is not generated. For example, someone can say that he is an honest person. But if at the first opportunity he lies, in reality his actions show that he is not honest.

When we are in a good mood, being kind is very easy, but when we are in a bad mood it is not so easy. So we have to show who we are in actions.

In this sense, motivation is very important—it is one thing to want something and quite another to achieve it. The link is motivation. Let's keep in mind that the motivation that really lasts is the internal one, the one that comes from *within*. And it always starts with a need. The need is something that, if someone does not have, dies or feels that it dies; it is not something optional.

Often, the motivation also comes from *outside*. For example: "I want that car and I will motivate myself to work until I buy it." For certain specific things, *external* motivation can be positive. However, when all our motivation comes from *outside*, it is because a sense of life and self has not been built inside. The reason that external motivation is not lasting is because, usually, after achieving the goal we wanted, we feel empty. Recovering from those gaps sometimes requires a lot of effort. The only way motivation creates constant fulfillment is if it comes from within.

How do we build internal motivation? Listening to what our being wants; connecting with ourselves. Ahead, we'll look at an exercise for doing that.

The reality is that the motivation of the vast majority of people is low and external. Unfortunately, people tend in general not to change until they hit rock bottom, until it becomes much more painful to stay put than to change.

The four horses

Buddhists explain that there are four types of people and compare them to four kinds of horses. They explain it in this parable:

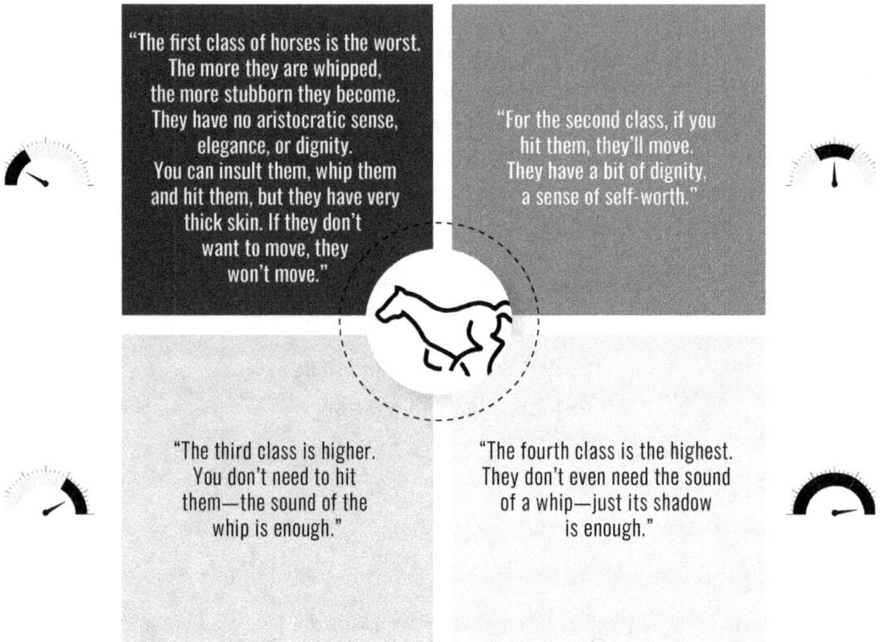

Emotionally mature people are those who act due to the mere suggestion of a crisis or a mistake. Those who navigate with low emotional intelligence don't act, even if they are presented with a terrible diagnosis, even their own death.

Many believe that some people are born more motivated than others. The reality is that, although we all had different examples and opportunities for motivation, we are all born with the same potential to act.

The six motivations

According to Tony Robbins, there are six needs by which human beings are motivated. The first four—**certainty**, **variety**, **meaning** and **love** and **connection**—are more linked to survival and are common and natural in the first years of life. When we reach adulthood without having fully satisfied these needs, we only move due to external motivation. The feelings of adults who are usually motivated by one of these four needs are generally fear, sadness or anger because their emptiness is usually a constant.

The last two—growth and contribution—are more abstract in nature, and unless a person begins an important reflection process, they will be incapable of realizing that these two needs are the only vehicles for human fulfillment. Ideally, an adult is motivated by either of these two.

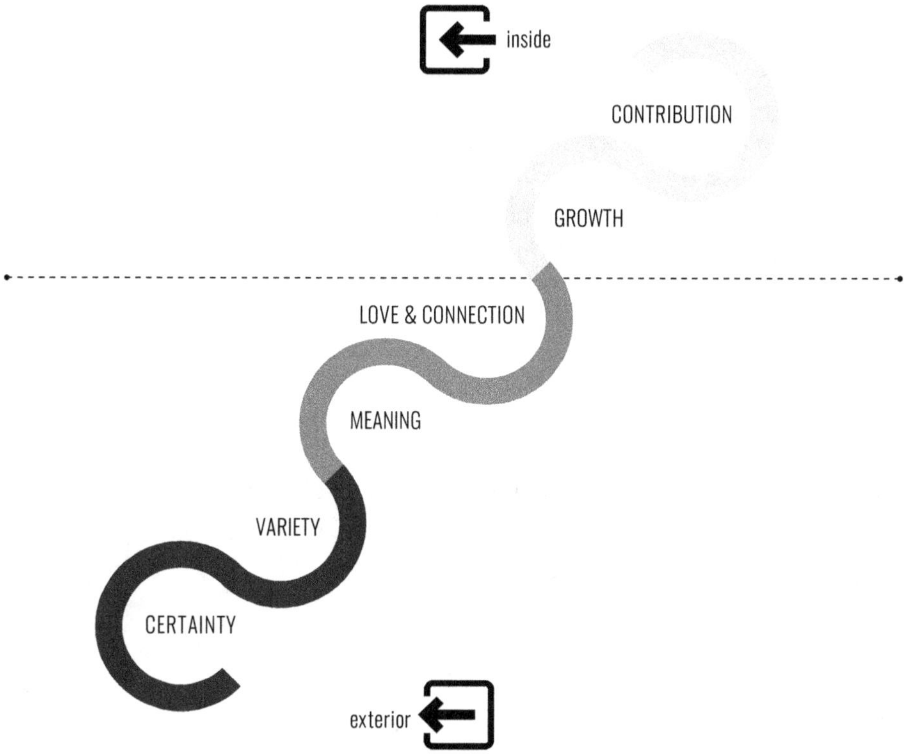

Certainty

This is the need to have a safe spot to deal with the great uncertainty that life represents. However, most of the things we create to feel certain exist only in our minds. Nothing is definite or stable, because everything changes. Certainty is different for each person. For some it may be something material and for others something emotional.

Some are obsessed with the security that money brings. Others are subject to God or religion. In the end, these are all *imaginary supports*, because money can be lost or kept, but it doesn't guarantee that an accident won't happen when you step out your door. Similarly, there are people who pray daily, for example, but still get Covid.

Experiencing certainty based on a **limiting belief** often means living with a great deal of apprehension about the basis of our belief; we may feel that we will die if the basis of our belief is not there. For example, there are people who go into a serious crisis when they lose their money or who feel extremely guilty when they fail to attend church.

But if we hold an **empowering belief**, we see money as a vehicle to improve our well-being. If we don't have money, there are other ways to generate that well-being. In other words, well-being is the important thing; money is just a tool to achieve it. The same with religion. Going to church can be a means of connecting with God, but it is not the connection itself. We can connect with God, or with our Higher Power, anytime and anywhere.

Variety

This is the opposite of certainty—the need to have new experiences, get out of our routine and break with the conventional. Variety, seen from a limiting perspective, can be exemplified by a person who decides to marry and live in monogamy, but still seeks sexual or romantic partners outside of marriage. The problem does not consist so much in having or not having different partners at the same time, but in maintaining a commitment to fidelity that is based on lies.

From an **empowering perspective**, the need for variety can be satisfied by learning new things, gaining new skills, breaking unproductive habits, or even letting go of destructive family traditions, such as codependency.

> Variety can help us evolve as people
> and to mature emotionally, as long as
> it is based on an empowering belief.

Meaning

This has to do with the need to be recognized socially, to feel important and to stand out from and be respected by our group. Behind this need, the person seeks *meaning*.

From a limiting perspective, seeking meaning can show itself as arrogance, "standing up" for things you do, competing destructively, obsessively seeking recognition, showing off and comparing yourself to others.

> Meaning from an empowering perspective
> is to add value to the world, to work
> to give more than we take, without
> necessarily having to be the boss.

Love and connection

The two most basic needs of human beings are love and belonging or connection. This has to do with our gregarious instinct—being part of a tribe.

Living these motivations from a limiting perspective is like saying "Hit me but don't leave me." It happens with people who prefer to live in a toxic relationship than to be alone. Or the opposite: they run away from relationships that add value for fear of abandonment, denying themselves love.

> Love and connection, from an
> empowering perspective, are allowing
> ourselves to be vulnerable, knowing
> how to ask for help, and appreciating
> the love that surrounds us.

Growth

This is the constant need to evolve. People driven by this motivation, even if they reach a goal that has involved significant effort, continue to seek growth.

> Real growth cannot be lived from
> a limiting perspective. It is always
> empowering. Growth will never destroy
> value. If it does, it wasn't about
> **growth**; it was about **variety**.

Contribution

This is the need to give in order to transform the world into a better place—an absolute and genuine service to others and to ourselves.

Contribution cannot be lived from
a limiting perspective either—it is
always empowering. Contribution will
never destroy value. If it does, it is
not **contribution**, but **meaning**

It is in the action, in our internal
sensation, and in the effect of
our action where we can truly see
which motivation is operative..

Our cousin Murray

Christmas 2007, Grandma's house

"Hey…my good-looking cousin Murray! How are you, how's it going?" A few months ago I heard that you started your own business. I want to know all about it!"

"Geez, my gorgeous cousin Sofia. You've missed knowing stuff that would be useful to any middling businessman. Basically, it's been a mega-challenge. To start from the beginning, I got connected with a French company that imports vehicles with special features—you know, for the disabled, for pregnant women and so on. You can imagine. Now we already have orders for staff at a hospital in the United States. Just imagine—we'll be the only company in the country providing this type of vehicle."

"That's good! I'm so happy for you, Murray. I bet in a few months you'll be so successful you won't even want to say hello to me, eh?"

"No way. I always try to be humble. Hey, maybe we'll even celebrate next Christmas in Switzerland, since Grandma's house will be too small for us."

Christmas 2008, Grandma's house

"Hello Sofia, Merry Christmas! Look at you, gorgeous as always. You still even look like a member of the family. Well…obviously, you're family. But before… you didn't like… um…well, you know! Hey, I've already had four whiskey sours!

"Merry Christmas, Murray. How are you? You didn't go to my sister's wedding. You must have been on business in France."

"Didn't they tell you? They really didn't tell you? I no longer have that nefarious vehicle business. It was exhausting to deal with customs. This country is super-corrupt. It doesn't understand anything about laws. My lawyers were in collusion with the government. A disaster. Now I have a new linen business for the five-star hotel industry. We bring the materials from Morocco, you know, the fabric; we embroider in it China; with Italian quality! It is quite a phenomenon. Most of the hotels in Cancun are our clients. They are super satisfied. This is the business, *dear* Sofia!

"I understand...I think. They're calling us for dinner, Murray."

"Sofia, we really have to say that this space is awful. Next year we can be in Tulum, in one of my friends' hotels.

Christmas 2009, Grandma's house

"Hello?"

"Sofia? It's me, Murray. No one answers the landline. I won't be able to get to grandma's house. My partner called me and said that one of the workers fell from the second floor. I'm super busy, you know... And they probably didn't tell you...I have a construction company.

"No, they didn't tell me. Merry Christmas Murray."

Our cousin Murray is a typical case of false self-esteem—in other words, someone who says that he is very good at something, but in action he can't prove it. Murray seems to believe, and is always saying, that he's a great businessman, but his results say otherwise.

> When we say that life happens in action,
> this means that if our results don't
> demonstrate what we say we are, then
> we are not what we say. Do your results
> corroborate what you say you are?

Help someone in need, anonymously. Often when we feel anxious, stressed, frustrated, confused or hurt, the best antidote is to reach out to help someone else. It may seem illogical to help someone when we feel bad ourselves, but, helping someone in need accomplishes two things:

1. We focus our attention on something that adds value, while we are healing our wound.

2. We "fill up our emotional tank" without resorting to control.

There is always someone who needs help—it's just a matter of observing your surroundings. If you can't find anyone in your immediate circle, like friends or family, look in a larger context, like your kids' school, your workplace, or your church. If you think that in your immediate circle you can't maintain anonymity, then consider more distant contexts, such as foundations or national and international public institutions.

The type of help you can offer ranges from leaving a note of encouragement on the desk of someone who is going through a difficult time, to participating in a volunteer program. The suggestion is to do it at least once a week, but the more complex your own current situation of anxiety or hurt, the more this helping exercise can assist you.

It is important, whatever help you give, that you remain anonymous. This ensures that the act of giving makes you feel whole and complete.

Often the line between helping and controlling is very thin—with anonymity we ensure that our giving is genuine.

You can share your experience in our group:
https://www.facebook.com/ddrmaru 

This exercise has been one of the most fulfilling and wonderful experiences for many of us.

6

LEVELS OF
CONSCIOUSNESS

Reflective thinking is the type that generates more personal growth. There are other types of thought that are also very valuable for human survival, such as creative or critical thought; however, reflective thinking is essential to find the meaning of existence and feel fulfilled.

Depending on how much we think reflectively, we can find ourselves in different states of consciousness. Although awareness is a deep and broad concept, here we will define it as **the ability to be aware of both my outer reality and my inner reality and to tell the difference**. Return to the introduction of this book if you need to recall what inner and outer realities are.

Human beings can navigate between different levels of consciousness in different aspects of our lives. In other words, in our relationships we may be more aware, while in finances our awareness is less. However, in general, a person is usually in very similar states of evolution of consciousness in all areas.

For example, it is very rare for someone to be at a very high level in love and very low in family; the difference either up or down will usually be one or two levels maximum. You may be more advanced in one area or another, but you are generally advancing at the same pace in most areas.

These levels of consciousness are:

- Unconsciousness
- Rebellion
- Paralysis
- Falsehood
- Courage
- Gratitude and appreciation
- Mindfulness or enlightenment

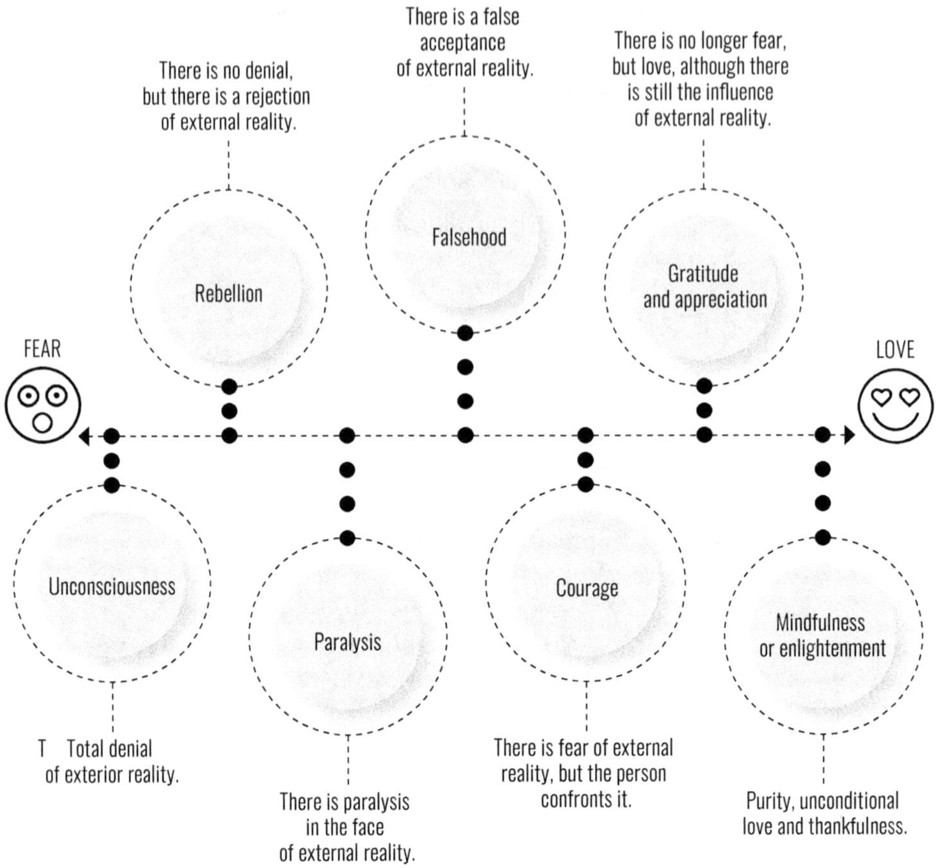

Unconsciousness

This is when a person does not make any contact with external reality; they deny verifiable facts that happen *outside* themselves.

Let us remember that we all eliminate and distort parts of reality, depending on our experience, education, religion, etc. But people in denial take this distortion to the limit.

To illustrate, we can posit an extreme situation. It is raining. But someone who is totally unconscious will deny this phenomenon even after they go outside and get soaked. They use no reflective thinking at all.

Rebellion

The person is no longer in total denial of the outside world, but rejects it, using illogical and non-reflective arguments to do so, and using the fantasy that rejection is going to eliminate external reality.

If it's raining, someone at this level says, "Yes, it's raining, but I don't want it to. Why does it rain, if I don't like it? I hate the rain..." and so on.

This person uses very little reflective thinking.

Although a person fights with the outside
world, kicks and throws a tantrum, he is
not going to modify an **exterior** fact.

Paralysis

People on this level remain motionless in the face of what happens outside. They don't know what to do; they go neither backwards or forwards.

When it rains, this person doesn't complain; he doesn't go out; he doesn't know whether to stay inside; he's on pause.

Reflective thought is
suspended, paralyzed.

Falsehood

The person's solution is to create a falsehood about an *outside* phenomenon.

Before rain, the person may claim he enjoys it, while inside rain really bothers him.

Reflective thought allows us to observe
our own real reactions, yet it may not
be strong enough to enable us to act
in accord with our observations.

Courage

As mentioned in another chapter, courage is facing something in spite of internal fear. At this level, the same thing happens when facing phenomena in the *external* world.

Perhaps a person is afraid of thunder or doesn't like to get wet, but if it is necessary to get drenched in order to accomplish an important goal or challenge a fear, the person would do so.

Reflective thought begins to be so
strong that it empowers the person.

Gratitude and Appreciation

A person feels much more gratitude and appreciation than fear of the *outside* world. Although generally the person's emotional state is love, external phenomena still affect him or her.

For example: "It's raining, and I appreciate this moment, even though getting wet is not one of my favorite experiences."

Mindfulness or enlightenment

This is the highest level reached by people who only feel love, gratitude and compassion towards the *outside* world. No phenomenon within external reality can disturb the emotional and psychological state of these people.

In the rain there is joy, love, gratitude and compassion, even if they get wet.

Reflective thinking is at its peak before,
during, and after an experience.

Volatile levels

This look at the spectrum can help us to know where we are in terms of our level of consciousness, and also to know where others are. Most people live on the first three rungs (unconsciousness, rejection, and paralysis).

This scale is a tool to feel love and compassion for ourselves as we learn to develop our reflective thinking and awareness. It also helps us to have a parameter with which to observe our progress towards the path of consciousness.

By understanding these levels, we can also understand other human beings and feel compassion because he or she is in a lower state of reflection. Maybe he's going about in **Falsehood**, but at least he's not in **Unawareness** or **Rebellion**.

It is natural that human beings experience a certain volatility in these levels, that we go from one to another in different areas of life. What is not natural is to be, for example, in **Gratitude** and **Appreciation** in several areas of life and in total **Unconsciousness** in only one, or in **Rebellion** in all areas and **Consciousness** in one.

Bouncing

If a person experiences regression from a state of higher reflective thought to lower, it is because he or she has not really changed. It is similar to what happens when you *rebound* during a diet: if someone's weight goes up and down, it is because the limiting belief that generates being overweight has not changed. He or she has not integrated the *outside* with the *inside*.

The faster we accept external reality,
the faster our evolution towards
consciousness and fulfillment will be.

80% of personal transformation work has to do with assimilating external reality; the other 20% is technical. Accepting the natural laws that we have talked about is one way of accepting external reality.

If what we really want is to stay comfortable (be stuck) where we are… well then…we must be willing to face the consequences of that decision. But it is important not to pretend that we are growing when in fact it is not true.

If we really want to evolve, it is essential to realize that every time we reject an aspect of external reality, we move backwards.

Personal transformation has to do with
restraining our denial, our rebellion,
our paralysis and our falsehood.

According to the Pan American Health Organization, in Latin America, about 50% of women who tolerate and do not report a situation of abuse have university studies and a good socioeconomic level (paho.org).

These women are generally in a state of **Falsehood** in which they repress pain and fear in order to maintain their status. In this case, the abuser is as responsible as the abused person, who negotiates her abuse in exchange for maintaining a false reputation.

Change and unconsciousness

Change is one of the most important concepts for human beings because the faster we adapt to it, the more chance we have not only of surviving, but of expanding our fulfillment in finances, love and health. On the contrary, if we resist change in life, we will find ourselves in serious trouble and will put ourselves and our loved ones at risk.

> All our problems come from resisting change, of not accepting what is new or different in external reality and of not letting go of our internal reality that clings to the past.

Our level of awareness is relative to our level of resistance to change. Another way to interpret the scale of consciousness is to see it as a scale of adaptation to change. The more we advance in the scale of consciousness, the more we can achieve success, health, love and better finances.

There are people who, despite the fact they are suffering, do not respond to all the help that is offered and are closed to receiving tools or accompaniment to feel better. They have great resistance to change because they are in a state of **Unconsciousness**. In these cases, unfortunately, the only thing that can be done is to wait until the person hits rock bottom, that is, until the pain of staying where they are is greater than the pain of changing. However, it is very important not to judge the person no matter how destructive their unconsciousness is. If, for example, a friend is allowing some kind of abuse by their partner in order to have financial security, our best choice may be to respect their process, to feel compassion and be ready to reach out when the person decides to wake up.

> Part of being an adult is assuming that victims don't exist, that everyone chooses and creates their own circumstances.

Take the leap

It is not possible to jump from one end of the scale to the other, for example, from a level of **Rejection to Acceptance**. It is necessary to pass through the different states. However, there are two exceptions:

- Experiencing a deeply **painful** event, such as a great loss

- Experiencing an event of deep **pleasure**, such as having an illuminating talk with the Dalai Lama

In these two ways, an awakening from **Unconsciousness** to **Consciousness** could occur. However, most human beings are not so receptive to experiences of such magnitude. There is a way to grow gradually, level by level.

> The most destructive thing for human development is **unconsciousness**.

To fly or not to fly

Jorge is a young man of 24 years; Since childhood, he had behavioral and learning problems. He never showed interest in any hobbies, sports or motivation. His parents own a helicopter hangar. Each missed school year was an opportunity for the parents to romanticize that their son would be the third pilot in the family.

"Is it Jorge who wants to be a pilot or is it you?" a therapist asked Jorge's mother.

Jorge attended primary school in six different schools, never at the academic level to which he belonged, yet his parents were certain that his intellect would advance. He was expelled from a public high school, which his mother put him into. Jorge did not feel the need for change, nor any economic pressure, nor even a small impulse to belong to a circle of friends.

"Jorge is disconnected from his school and his environment because you, his parents, are disconnected from him," another specialist explained.

Jorge cut short his high school education and his parents sent him to Canada, imagining that the problems would cease in a different geographical environment. But after a few months, the young man was back in the family nest—his personality was not moving towards responsibility.

"What is it that prevents you from seeing Jorge as he is? asked a psychologist.

Jorge's mother had the hope deep down that her son would one day become a pilot—and that way she would always have him close. Bills for specialists in mental disorders were rising, and the desperate mother enrolled Jorge in a private school for pilots in the city of Querétaro, without encouraging results.

"Distortion is the main mechanism by which human perception misrepresents external reality," said a book.

Jorge's adult working life has been as a waiter, security guard and bagger, never as a pilot. But despite the innumerable evidence that Jorge's life gives his mother, she continues to insist that her son will one day be a pilot and that she will always have him by her side.

"Having the ability to observe reality is a great virtue," said another book.

Jorge's mother has suffered and will continue to suffer frustration and pain because her son, after all the opportunities he's had, chose to be a "nobody." The question: where does the suffering of the mother come from? From Jorge and his apathy? The answer: no.

Suffering comes from the inability to be aware of reality, to keep insisting on distorting over and over what continues to happen daily under one's nose.

Exercises

Step 1

Identify where you are on the scale of consciousness. Trying to be very objective, answer the following question with total honesty:

When I find myself in a situation that challenges me personally or professionally, my initial reaction is:

a) Complain and get angry. It really shocks me that things don't turn out the way I expect. Often, raising my voice and making it clear who I am is the only way to get things resolved.

b) I freeze and don't know what to do. I have no idea what to do or where to start. Often, it is better not to do anything and wait for someone else to solve the problem or for the situation to change.

c) I say everything is under control, but in reality I feel a lot of stress. I don't want others to realize that I'm not having a good time.

d) Even with all the stress that can be generated, I take immediate action to face the matter or solve the problem. I express my stress and frustration and deal with it in the best possible way.

e) I really stress very little, but not because I don't care. On the contrary, I know that behind every challenge there is great learning opportunity and I feel gratitude. Generally, with calm and mental clarity, I perceive many possibilities and choose the one that brings the greatest benefit to myself and those around me.

Ask people from different areas of life (your family, friends, partner, work, sports team, etc.) to share with you how they perceive you, using the above question.

Compare your answers with theirs. The item that is repeated the most is probably the state of consciousness in which you find yourself.

Interpretation of results:

- If you had a majority saying **a**, it is likely that you are in a **Rejection** state.

- If you had a majority saying **b**, you are probably in a state of Paralysis.

- If you had a majority saying **c**, it is likely that you are in a state of **Falsehood**.

- If you had a majority saying **d**, it is likely that you are in a state of **Courage**.

- If you had a majority saying **e**, you are probably in a state of **Gratitude**.

> Nota: This survey does not explore the state of Unconsciousness or Full Consciousness. In Unconsciousness, this exercise is not effective because the person does not have the resources to observe himself. On the other hand, the number of people in Full Consciousness is very small.

Step 2

Implement the strategy that will take you to the next level. Once we identify what level we are at, the question is, what to do to grow?

If you are in Rejection or Paralysis, you can keep a diary. In every challenging situation, ask yourself (or ask someone you trust to help you answer):

- Do I want others to see me like this?

- What will others think if things continue like this?

- Would I rather stay like this and not be prepared for a real crisis?

- Would I like to see a person I love in this state?

If you are in **Falsehood** or **Bravery** you can keep a diary and, in each challenging situation, ask yourself:

- What am I afraid of?
- What is the worst thing about this situation and this fear?
- What do I feel I lose if I accept this situation?

If you are in **Gratitude** you can continue to expand your state with any of these guided meditations, and also do the previous written exercises for any of the other states.

7

EMOTIONS OF
CONTROL

Emotions are not strange entities that affect us. They occur inside our bodies in certain situations.

Just as we human beings have forms of communication, whether with words, gestures, written language or even silence, the body also has channels to express itself. This happens in three ways, resulting from hormones and neurotransmitters that our body generates in the face of certain situations:

- Pressure changes
- Movement
- Temperature changes

We can describe the former as a type of pain or discomfort; For example: "I feel empty in my stomach," "I feel a lump in my throat" or "I feel like my shoulders weigh a ton." If we pay close attention to the sensation, we will even discover that the change in pressure can be from the inside out or from the outside in.

The movement can take many forms, from involuntary muscle contractions to chills.

Changes in temperature can be exemplified by that heat we feel in our cheeks when we feel anger or with a cooling of our hands when we experience fear.

These three factors in combination, or sometimes alone, are the ways in which the body speaks to us.

To listen to this language we must be
attentive without judging, since the
channels are associated with pain.

Emotional

There are two types of emotional energy: one that builds and one that destroys, depending on the training we have in managing emotions. We can experience unpleasant emotions that do not necessarily become destructive if we learn to channel them.

The root of all emotions is the same, only we turn it into something specific. This is like Newton's experiment where a ray of light passes through a prism and diffracts into the different colors of the rainbow—just like on the cover of Pink Floyd's "The Dark Side of the Moon" album.

The energy is one, but it can be expressed
in pleasant or unpleasant emotions;
we are the prism that diversifies it.
It is up to us to channel emotions in
a constructive or destructive way.

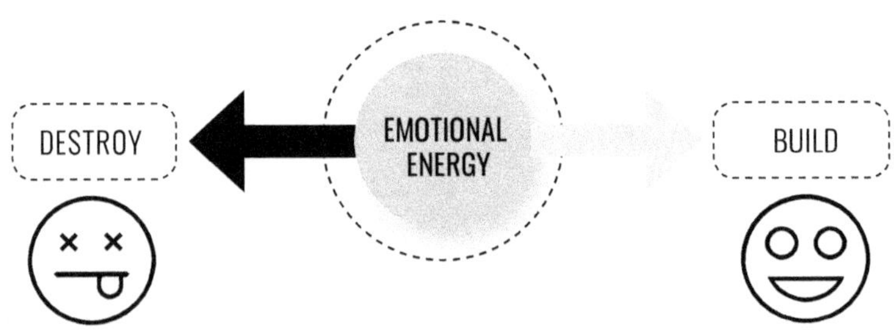

Two emotional paths

Developing the ability to channel emotions takes a lot of practice as we become mindful. Ideally, we should be taught this skill from a young age, but most of us reach adulthood without developing it.

> The nature of each emotion is always good; it becomes productive or destructive depending on how we filter it.

We call the energy that becomes productive the **emotions of being**, which are conscious reactions resulting from **empowering** beliefs.

When the energy becomes destructive, we call them **control emotions**, which are a visceral reaction, the result of **limiting** beliefs.

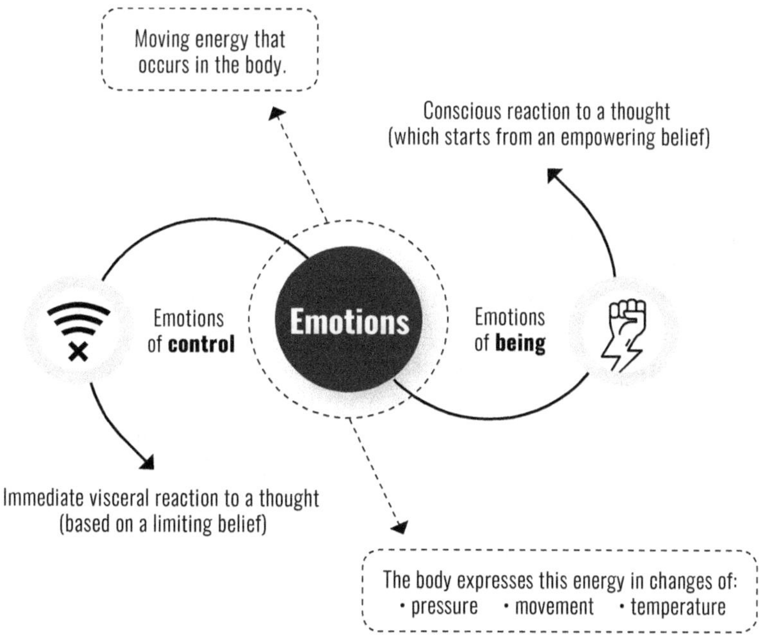

Emotions of control

By experiencing **emotions of being** we are already empowering ourselves. Problems can start when we experience the other types.

Emotions of control manifest when there is a perception that our inner reality is different from our outer reality, and this difference is seen from within a **limiting** belief that leads us to think that instead of changing ourselves, we should change the world.

Every time we set out to modify the ***outside*** world and don't analyze how to transform our ***interior*** world, an **emotion of control** is generated.

In turn, there are two types of emotions of control, based on how much we express those emotions:

- Repressed control

- Expressed control

Repressed control

This is the emotion that arises when we need something from *outside* in order to be well. This tends to be anger and is called repressed control because we just feel the emotion, but don't express it. Sometimes the opposite emotion is even expressed as long as no one realizes what we are feeling.

Often the emotion of control occurs without us realizing it—unconsciously, so we are not even able to detect the changes in pressure, movement or temperature that the body generates to indicate that there is a need to control.

Expressed control

This also arises when there is a need to change something on the *outside* to be well. But here we don't repress the emotion, but express it—we let it out like a pressure cooker that can no longer contain the steam. We *explode*— sometimes because we've held back for so long, sometimes because we have the fantasy that with our scream or fists we'll make another person change.

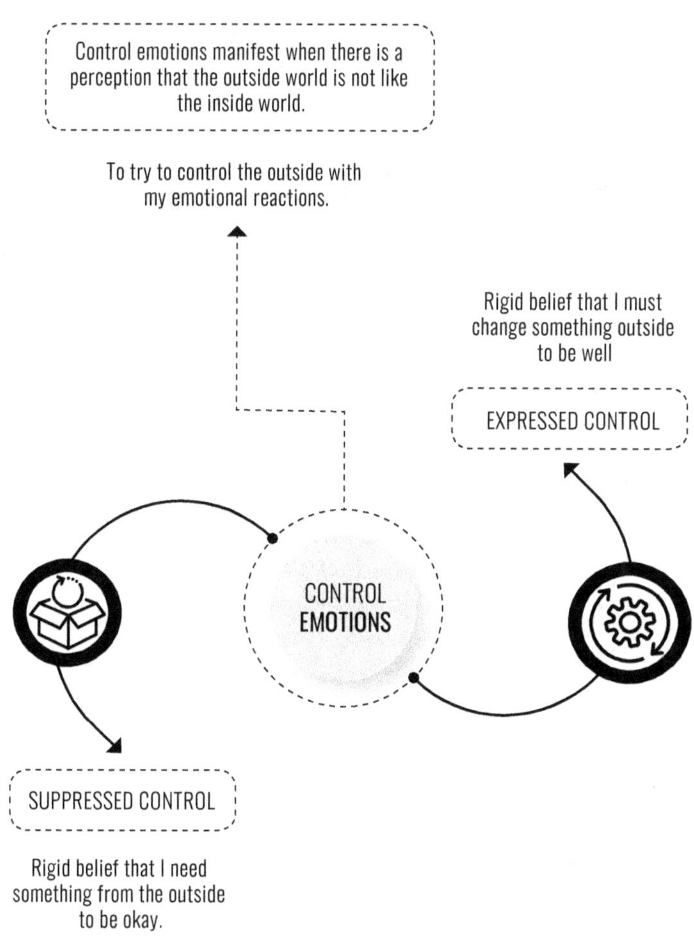

Families of control

We can relate the concept of the **emotion of control** to the types or families of emotions that we have already seen in a previous chapter. These are called **primary emotions**, because even animals can experience them even though they are poorly elaborated.

Every time we feel an **unpleasant** emotion that becomes destructive, it is an **emotion of control**, and the language of our body manifests itself in an unpleasant way. These are, specifically: anger, fear and sadness.

Experiencing any of these three emotions indicates a *disconnection* between what is *inside* and what is *outside*. In other words, we try to change the world instead of changing ourselves, try to wash our hands of responsibility for what we feel, and we blame external reality.

EMOTION	CAUSE	SUGGESTED ACTION TO AVOID CONTROL
Anger	External threat to our image. Something throws into doubt what we think we are. The more rigid the image is, the greater the anger.	Identify and let go of any false image of what we pretend to be.
Fear	Lack of data (fear of unknown or lack of experience).	Reflect: What question should we ask ourselves to solve a problem?
Sadness	Impotence—the world is not as we'd like	Accept the loss and/or accept the situation as it is.

Emotional states derived from not knowing how to handle emotions of control

Depression

This is a recurrent, total and **unconscious** disconnection from our ability to adapt and change. In this state, we feel that we cannot do anything to transform our **inner reality**. When we are in depression, we choose the role of victims to obtain a benefit. This is also a self injury that has been repressed for a long time.

Anxiety

This is the result of not identifying and channeling fear for a long time. Generally, it results from having narrow thought patterns in the face of possible new experiences; in other words, thoughts that do not see the whole, but only focus on the negative. Some types of thoughts that cause anxiety are: fatalistic thoughts about the immediate or long-term future ("I'm sure my boss called me to his office because he's going to fire me"), generalizing an experience ("Since they fired Marimar yesterday, today they'll fire me") or *predicting* the future without cause ("I just have a hunch that now they're going to fire me.")

Boredom

This is a total disconnect from ourselves due to a 100% focus on **external reality**. It is when we pretend that what is outside is entertaining us, forgetting what is *inside* and our responsibility for our **inner reality.** It is a complete lack of respect for being alive, considering that in reality there are thousands of things happening in the world, and it is up to us to explore them.

Expensive angel

Monday

Pearl was sure she was an angel. Just as she did at the beginning of every week, she got up to make the food that her brother, Joaquin, would take to work. She was an excellent cook; she had taken gastronomy courses to delight her family. When everything was ready, she put the food in his lunch box and added a note: "Bon appétit."

Joaquin took the food hurriedly, said a short "thank you" to Perla and hurried away. He knew that those delicacies would cost him dearly.

Tuesday

The car belonging to Jessica, Perla's niece, had broken down, and Perla, as the good aunt, offered her car so that Jessica wouldn't have to travel by subway.

"With this pandemic, I don't want you riding public transport."

"No, Aunt Pearl, seriously, I can take an Uber."

"No way. Here, take the keys. Or is my car too ugly for you?" Pearl insisted.

Jessica reluctantly agreed, even though she knew it would cost her dearly.

Wednesday

The phone rang. When Perla answered, a recording told her that Maria, her sister-in-law, had fallen behind on her credit card payment. After hanging up, Perla took her cell phone and made an electronic transfer to settle her debt.

When Maria found out, she was worried. The payment was small, but it would be expensive for her.

Thursday

Perla arranged to help all day in her neighbor's restaurant, whose staffers had quit. Even though the owner of the place tried to politely refuse the help, there was no human power that could dissuade Pearl.

"That woman is an angel," one of the diners said. "Perlita is always helping everyone."

An expensive angel, the neighbor thought.

Friday

When the weekend approached, it was time for Perla to collect. Every Friday she got sick from something, and began to exercise control emotions towards others, charging them for all the favors she had done for them during the week. She used blackmail, whining and appeals to pity.

Her friends and her family were getting fed up, since every Friday Perla's blood pressure went up, she got Covid, her blood sugar spiked or her head hurt. She tried to appeal to other people's guilt.

Everyone got together with Perla to eat and see if she recovered from her ills, because they felt indebted to her. But watch out not to refuse anything Perla wanted, because then she gets into her passive aggression.

Pearl was the queen of the weekend, convinced that she was an angel, an expensive angel.

Although the emotions of control can make the world fall at our feet and do what we want at the moment, they are very expensive, both for the person who generates them and for those who receive them.

Control invariably breeds pain and destruction, even when disguised as kindness. The only thing that sustains true and nurturing relationships **is** love.

Exercises

Emotional diary 3

This diary consists of keeping track of our emotions within the following structure:

Step 1

Describe the real-life situation in which you are experiencing a disagreeable emotion.

Step 2

What kind of emotion did you have?

a) **Repressed control**

- What do you want to change on the outside (in exterior reality)?

- What do you fear losing in this situation?

b) **Expressed control**

- What are you trying to control on the outside (in exterior reality)?

- What emotion did you use (sadness, anger or fear)?
- What did you hope to accomplish with that emotion?

Step 3

What is a better way to achieve your objective?

8

THE PAIN OF
GROWTH

Real growth is free of ego. As we have already said, in life there are two ways of acting: **intelligent actions** and **habitual actions**. The former guarantees evolution and change; the latter refer to always doing the same thing without question.

For our actions to be intelligent, we must ensure that they come from a real need for **growth** and **contribution**. If our actions start from any of the other needs that we have already talked about (certainty, variety, meaning, love and connection) there will be no guarantee of reaching a transformation.

No human being moves if he
does not have a real need.

Pain

The pain is a firing of the nerves of the body. That shot can be felt in three different ways: as a change in **pressure**, or a change in **temperature**, or **movement**. We sometimes label as pain these sensations of pressure, temperature, or movement. If we remove the label, we realize that we are only experiencing these three types of sensations that can sometimes be uncomfortable. For example, a backache is really a pressure on the back, a chill is a change in temperature and also a movement.

Sometimes, the pain is not only physical, but also emotional, and it manifests itself in three ways: **with anger**, **sadness** or **fear**. Regardless of whether these three emotions can be uncomfortable, only if we label them as something bad will they make us suffer. For example, when we fail in a project that we were excited about, we are likely to feel sadness or anger because of the pain of not having achieved the goal.

> For the human being, pain is a
> key concept because there is
> no growth without pain.

A painless experience does not lead to growth, and this has nothing to do with masochism. Pain has no connotation, neither positive nor negative, although socially, negative prejudices have been imposed on it.

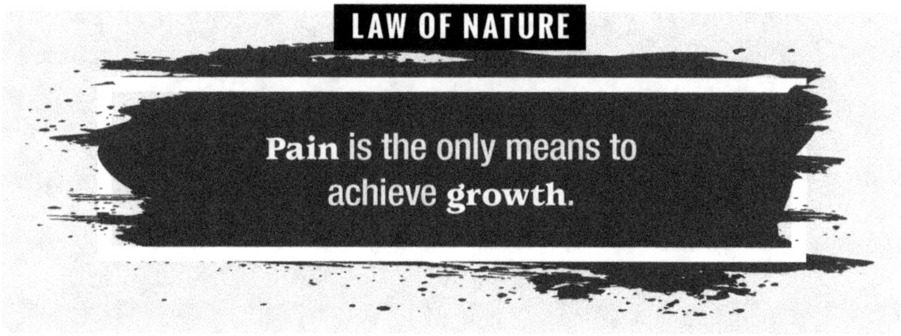

The previous statement may seem offensive, but this is only a stigma. There are many pains that are socially accepted; for example, in Mexico, eating food loaded with hot chiles produces joy, although this is a nervous reaction to the irritation produced by the chili's capsaicin. Nobody attaches the label of pain to this, even though it is. The more we consume this substance, the more we generate resistance—in other words, we increase the pain threshold.

Exercising is another way to enjoy pain—what happens is that muscle fibers tear at a microscopic level and lactic acid is produced, which is often uncomfortable.

It is sometimes said "No pain, no gain."
The same thing applies to growth.

Insensitive

There is a condition called congenital insensitivity to pain with anhidrosis (CIPA); the nerves of those who suffer from it do not fire when hit with pain. Most of these people die very young because their body is not able to react to the small pains that precede, for example, the ejection of urine or feces, nor to symptoms of something serious. There is even an episode in the series "*Dr. House*" that deals with this condition.

Physical pain and emotional pain

Physical pain is a survival tool because it alerts us to situations that harm the body; ignoring it can take us to the extreme of a serious illness, losing a limb or even dying.

Emotional pain is also a tool that helps us identify the values with which we want to navigate our lives. In the emotional realm, we need to feel a lot of pain about something in order to know that something is very important in our lives and is one of our priorities.

> What hurts us the most is what matters
> most to us; it is our maximum value.

This is different for each person. Money hurts some, love hurts others, health hurts others—it depends on what pain teaches each of us at different times. If we ignore a painful warning signal, we miss what interests us most, our priority, what we came into the world to do.

Yet, whether physical or emotional pain, there is a social aversion and stigma attached to pain. What society ignores is that the more we try to avoid pain, the more we put our lives at risk, and the more we lose track of where we are going and who we are.

We must remove the value judgment from pain and make it our *coach*, since pain—physical or emotional—allows us to identify if there is a problem and how to solve it. Pain and fulfillment are two sides of the same coin.

Confusion between physical and emotional pain

Excessive value judgments against pain has also caused us confusion in distinguishing between physical and emotional pain. The physical, in certain situations, could be a sign that our life is in danger, but the emotional, no matter how intense it may be, will never lead us to death, unless we choose to die. For example, people who have died *out of spite* were actually killed by the way they reacted to the loss.

If we react with emotional intelligence, it is more difficult for emotional pain, however extreme it may be, to extinguish our lives. This is the reason why many people do not face certain situations in life that involve being emotionally hurt, such as having a partner or starting a business—they falsely believe that a broken heart will end their lives.

If we human beings let go of the mistaken
idea that emotional pain operates
like physical pain, we would open
ourselves to revealing the possibility
of **failure**, among other things.

Failure is one of the main causes of emotional pain, but if we approach it with reflective thinking and empowering beliefs, it can lead to **growth**.

In the same way that physical pain, after going to the gym, causes our muscles to grow, emotional pain will lead to a real growth of our consciousness and power.

To believe that there is growth
without failure is a fantasy.

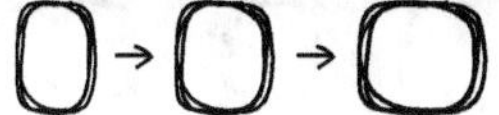

A successful entrepreneur has learned through the fall of five other companies; a functional couple is only functional thanks to their past failures; an Olympic champ has been in second place a thousand times.

Pain and suffering

Pain isn't optional, suffering is. Physical pain is a survival mechanism, whereas emotional pain is a mechanism to connect with ourselves. The only way of avoiding feeling pain is being dead.

	NON-OPTIONAL/NATURAL	OPTIONAL/ARTIFICIAL
PAIN Bullet shot on your body's nerves	X	
SUFFERING Intellectual and emotional projection		X
CHANGE	X	
GROWTH Implies pain + effort + increases margin of options		X

Suffering is a social interpretation which assumes pain as something bad. In practice, suffering is an **unconscious** strategy of control which tries to reject pain; however, on the contrary, what it does is intensify it.

For decades, emotional education in Latin America, and especially in Mexico, has been taught by telenovelas and ranchera songs, in which suffering is used time and again as a mechanism of manipulation and social connection.

A lot of reflective thought is necessary for us to open ourselves to pain and not to fall into suffering, which is a fanciful and vain defense system to avoid pain.

The time and care that emotional and physical scars require in order to heal depends on their gravity. If a wound remains open for years and years, not only does it imply that we haven't dedicated the necessary amount of self care, it also shows that we have chosen to suffer. This is the case for people who have stopped speaking to their relatives for 20 or 30 years, just because of "what they have done to them."

Suffering does not make wounds close. On the contrary, it makes them get infected, even to the point that we may lose a limb. The same thing happens with emotions. The longer it takes us to seek help, the more our psychological chaos will be.

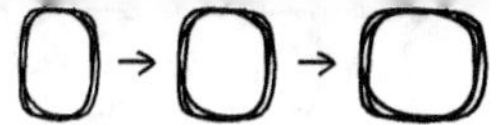

Change hurts

Every time there is change, there is pain. It's useless to think that we can evolve without transforming ourselves, that is, without pain. If we want to have more money, better health and more love, we must disconnect from our I, which produces very little, and then build up an I that would generate more—and this hurts.

Potential growth is directly
proportional to pain

Growth = Effort + Results.

Growth is optional and artificial, which means that not everything that hurts us becomes growth. In order to grow, we must invest effort and verify that it is generating the results we are looking for in an effective way. When facing change, some people choose to grow Others choose just to put in effort without achieving ideal results, and some others, choose only to suffer and die. Change itself, for example, losing a home after an earthquake may represent an opportunity to get a better and bigger house for some people. For others, it may be a reason to sink into an addiction or to get lost in shame and sorrow.

Suffering is a personal decision.

To move on or remain stuck implies equal effort—the difference is in the results themselves. A decision to be born (or not to be born) is not under discussion here. A decision to enter or not into life is out of the question—we're already aboard this train. We can't hit pause or rewind—so it's better to choose to grow.

We are free to choose suffering, and like everything else, there isn't bad or evil, we must just be aware of the decision we take and the consequences that come with it.

Suffering in Latin America

Suffering in Latin America gives rise to a great benefit: it attracts the attention of other people. Despite the great qualities of Latino culture, one of its biggest flaws is the fact that suffering is not only a habit but also a means of social cohesion. Those who suffer more are those who receive more attention. There is a point where it seems like a competition is being held to see who can suffer the most. This is one of the many reasons why Latin America is one of the regions in the world with the least progress.

To produce or not to produce

From the point of view of growth, there are two types of people:

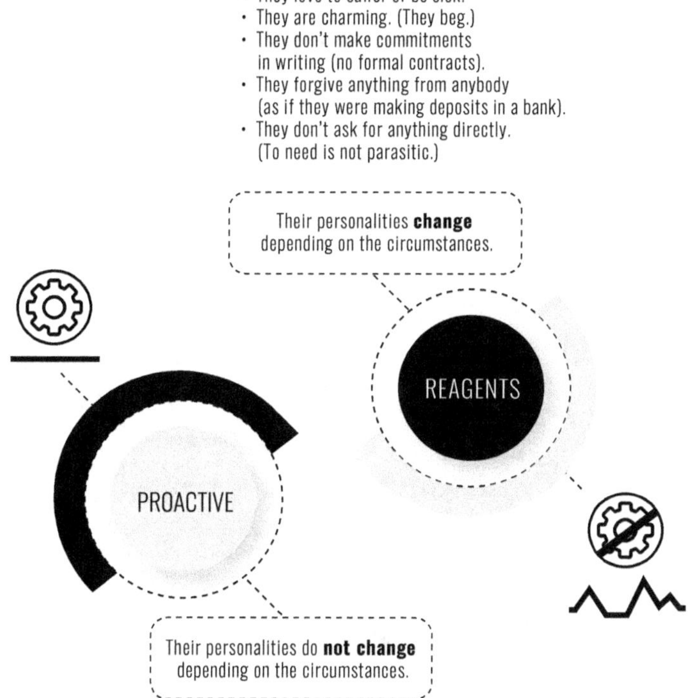

The **proactive** type of person provides a higher amount of value to the world compared to the amount they take from it. The **reactive** type takes away more value than what they give. Proactive people grow; reactive people don't.

A way to distinguish between people who grow and people who pretend to grow is that **proactive** people do not alter their personality in the face of circumstances. This means that it doesn't matter how strong the storm may be, they will always be kind, resilient and will put forth effort.

Reactive people don't grow; they just pretend to grow. They change their personality in regard to circumstances; if everything goes well, the person is well, but if something goes wrong, the person becomes a monster, suffering all the time, not keeping their word, and not accepting commitment. Such people would forgive anything just so they can accuse others afterwards using their secret discontent. They don't ask for things directly, don't ask for help and tend to use emotional blackmailing. Such people do not accept pain.

Ego and consciousness

Let's remember that as human beings we have both an inner reality and an outer reality, one inside and another one outside.

Our consciousness is the capacity to observe outer reality. The opposite is the ego, which separates us from outer reality and leads us to distort it. The bigger the ego, the less consciousness.

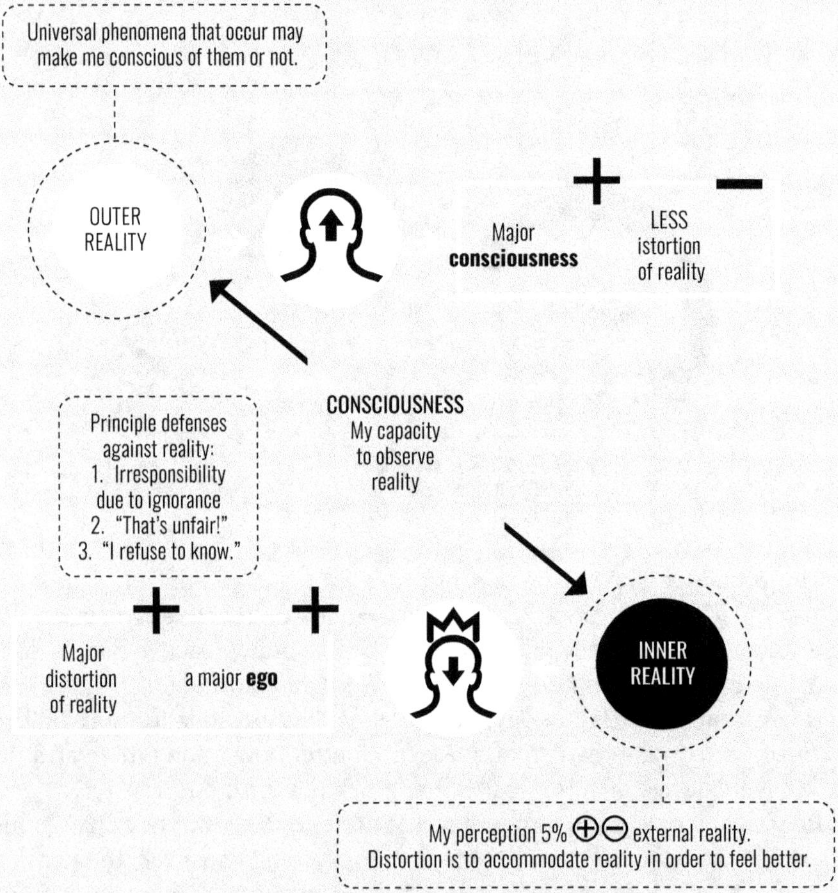

Universal phenomena that occur may make me conscious of them or not.

OUTER REALITY

+ Major **consciousness**

− LESS istortion of reality

CONSCIOUSNESS
My capacity to observe reality

Principle defenses against reality:
1. Irresponsibility due to ignorance
2. "That's unfair!"
3. "I refuse to know."

+ Major distortion of reality

+ a major **ego**

INNER REALITY

My perception 5% ⊕⊖ external reality.
Distortion is to accommodate reality in order to feel better.

DISTORTION: Main mechanism of human perception
TYPES OF DISTORTION: Annihilation, fabrication, synthesis and generalization

The distance of pain

One kilometer, 20 blocks, 20 minutes in the city

The alarm clock rang at 5:15 a.m. The insomnia from the night before hadn't allowed me to sleep till 1:30 a.m. My first job interview is at 8:30. I have memorized my goals as a professional. I have printed copies of my excellent grades from the last two semesters. I bought myself a new pair of shoes and I brought that letter of recommendation which could get me the position. Traffic is slow. I just took two wrong turns, parked my car and ran to the office building. By the time I arrived, my esophagus was hurting. My contract was set up for three years. Being the assistant to the financial manager helped to familiarize me with the restaurant sector.

Three kilometers, Mexico City marathon, 35 minutes

I had been training for a month, twice a week. I thought five kilometers would be easy. It began at 7:00 a.m. The night before I went to bed early, but next morning I had a fever and was shivering. At 6:30 a.m. I was on the starting line. Halfway through, my left knee started shaking. I had a slight pain, as if a screw had been loosened up, and then, I collapsed. I don't know how what happened—a day earlier I had felt no pain at all. I stopped running for some months for fear of feeling the same pain in my knee again.

**Pain is not optional. The amount
of suffering may vary, but we
cannot avoid it completely.**

Five kilometers, a gym in Mexico City

I ran into an old schoolmate. We met a few days to have a cup of coffee. He pitched me the possibility of opening a small business of promotional articles for coffee shops. He would put up the office; I would put up part of the capital, my car and my computer equipment as assets for our company. We were business partners for a year. One afternoon, the National Commission of Water asked us for an estimate for a campaign. They wouldn't pay us until 10 months later, and our investment would be huge. After winning the project, I was depressed for a week, had a backache that wouldn't let me go to the office, and a morning migraine that wouldn't allow me to even think about my physical state. A day later, I went to the gym to run. It only took four kilometers to realize that I wasn't prepared, and fear...

…would prevent me from continuing with the company that had cost me so much to start.

But we're also capable of feeling
emotional pain, which doesn't
kill us, no matter how hard and
deep the wound may be.

200 meters, the offices of Hultz, Human Resources

I exited the subway station and walked just a few blocks to my job interview, then waited a half an hour in the lobby. My hands got clammy and it was hard to breathe. I started to sweat. I went to the receptionist and asked her to reschedule my appointment for another day. I had a stomach ache.

The reason we don't grow and that we continue for years in the same situation, the same toxic relationship, the same obesity or the same financial issues is because we do not want to expose ourselves to pain, which can manifest itself in many ways: stomach pain, cold sweaty hands, fear of losing an entire investment, and so on. By saving minutes or days of pain, we lose a lifetime of fulfillment.

Potential growth is directly
proportional to pain.

Growth = Effort + Results.

Responsibility journal

This journal serves to verify if we really are on the right track. towards growth through intelligent action. It also serves to connect with ourselves.

We can use this journal every day to analyze the situations of each day, or if we have a serious problem of some sort.

STEP 1

Answer the next questions with brief, concrete sentences.

- What is today's problem?
- How do I describe this situation?

STEP 2

Answer the next questions with a brief phrase:

- Considering that I am the only person responsible for what is going on with me, how did I put myself in this situation or how did I trigger this problem?

STEP 3

Answer the next question with a brief phrase:

- If I had a magic wand, what would I want today's reality to be?

STEP 4

Answer the next questions with a brief phrase:

- Why don't I feel complete?

- What is it that I believe I lack from the outside world that would make me feel complete?

STEP 5

Answer the next question with a brief phrase:

- Do I really recognize that this situation or issue originated from my limited beliefs and that they are not caused by the exterior world?

STEP 6

If the previous questions have not resolved the inner conflict, explore the next questions:

- What do I get if I decide to keep the situation as it is today?

- Why do I choose to perpetuate this problem?

- What is it that I'm missing that makes me cover up, ignore or avoid this situation?

- Do I really recognize that this situation or issue originated in my limited beliefs and that they are not being caused from outside?

9

TYPES OF
IDENTITY

Our identity is how we define and see ourselves. Sometimes our identity can drive and motivate us to achieve what we want, and sometimes, it may limit us too. For example, if we think that we are good at studying, and that we also come from a family of *intellectuals* where we *easily* learn, then study will be easy for us. But if, on the contrary, our identity is built on ideas such as "This thing called school was not made for me" or "I'm stupid," then it will take us much more effort to be good learners.

Identity types are a mental map that allows us to see if our identity helps or hinders us from the path to fulfillment and success.

A mental map is not identical to reality; it is an abstraction of reality. These mental maps serve as compasses to guide us in building an internal order within the chaos and the great uncertainty of reality when our consciousness is not fully developed. This is why mental maps are associated with success—because they generate an order that, although fictitious and temporary, considerably reduces anxiety.

To be, to do and to have

Identity types are, at the same time, within another major mental map denominated as To be, to do, and to have. This map classifies people's experiences into three types:

- **To have**: when people feel their level or worth lies in possessing things or people.

- **To do**: when people feel their level of worth lies on how useful they are (how many things they do and how well they do them).

- **To be**: When people feel their level of worth is superior regardless of what they have or what they do.

The unconscious

It is important to know that our identity, like most of our tools and obstacles, lives in our unconscious. The human psyche is like an iceberg: 90 percent of it is under water and 10 percent above the surface; that is, that 90 percent of our perceptions and reasons for our behavior are submerged in the unconscious.

There are many aspects that operate in our life, but we do not realize it; however, not seeing them does not mean that they don't influence our actions.

The following scheme is known as the Johari Window (for its creators: Joseph Luft and Harry Ingham), and illustrates how there are aspects of ourselves that we do not know (unconscious) and aspects that we know (conscious):

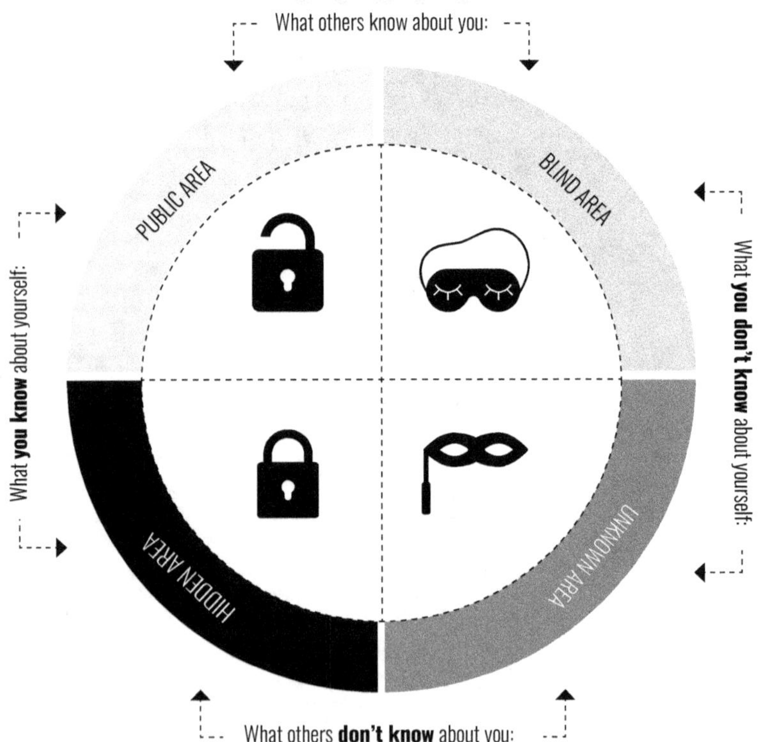

-  The **public area** is what I know about myself and is also known by others.

- The **blind area** is what I don't know about myself but others see.

-  The **hidden area** is what I know about myself but others don't know.

-  The **unknown area** is what neither I nor others know about me, but which exists even though nobody can see it.

Revealing what we don't know leads us to growth; and moving what we don't see into the visible areas leads us to personal development.

Reflective thought is the tool to make conscious the unknown or unconscious aspects of ourselves.

Types of Identity

This mental map, then, shows where the person deposits his or her identity. The types of identity are:

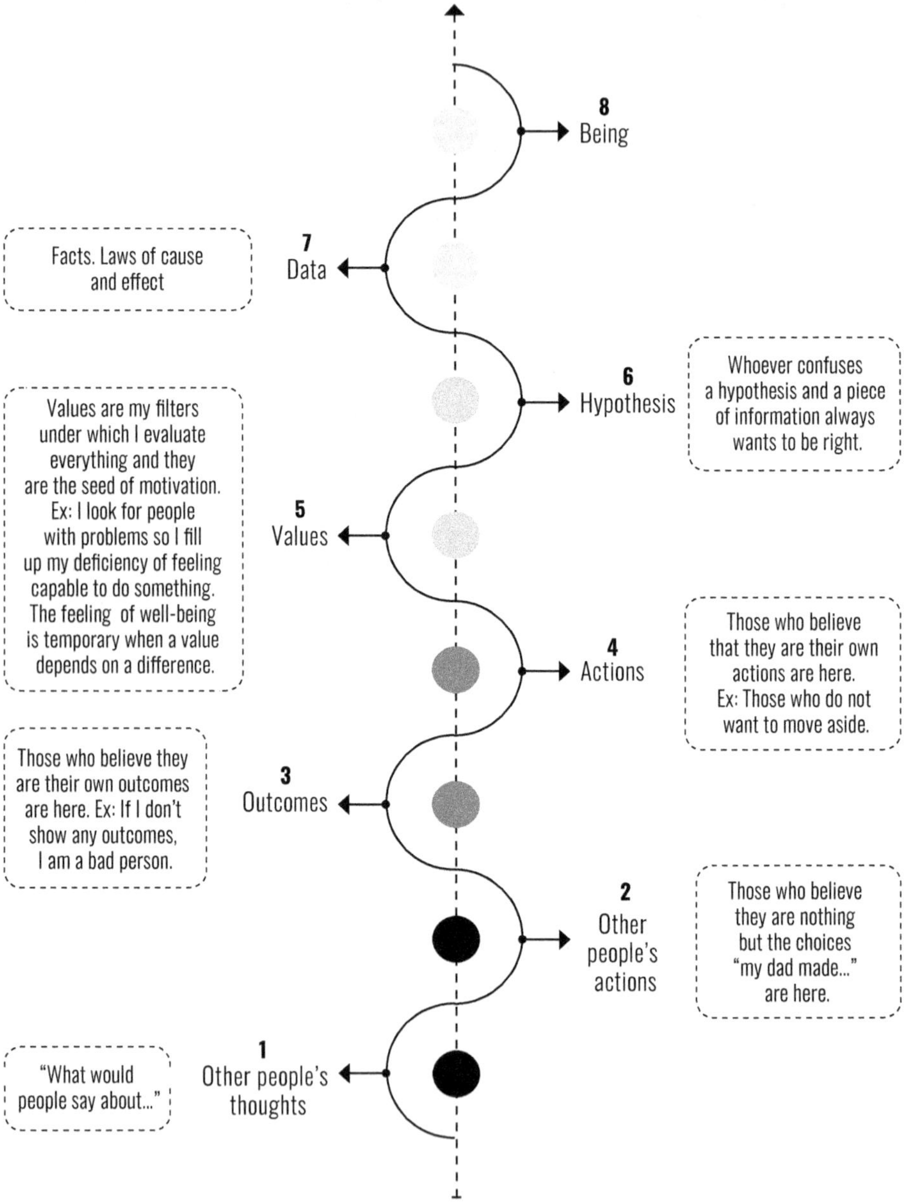

Identity 1. I am what other people think about me.

There are people who think they're what others think of them, that their worth depends on the perception of others. Those who belong to this point live in dependence on "what others will say" (with very little reflective thought).

Identity 2. I am what others do.

People who think that their value and identity are rooted in the actions of others. For example, they believe that if a family member, or a person very close to them, has committed a crime, they are the same. They may believe that they are criminals themselves (with little reflective thinking).

Identity 3. I am my outcomes.

People who think that their success or failures define them. When they do something right, they feel great, but when something goes wrong, they feel terrible. They have volatile emotions and run away from failure. This is a type of identity typical of people who experience themselves based on what they have.

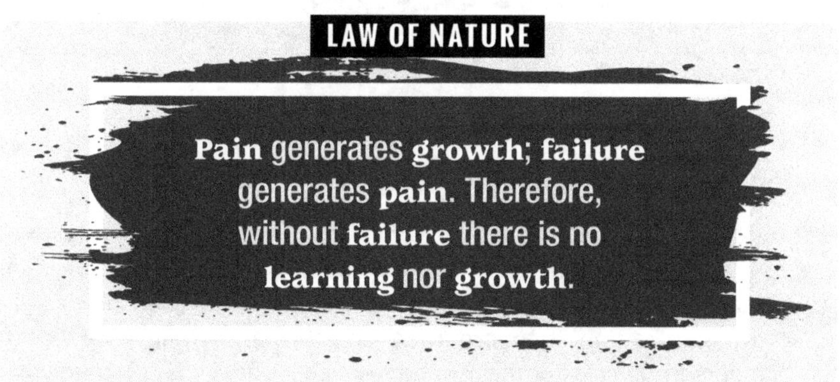

Identity 4. I am my actions.

Those who believe that they are their actions are the classic example of people who are confused about *doing*. A typical case is a retiree who becomes very depressed when they stop working.

Identity 5. I am my values.

These people think their values equate to absolute truth. For example, there are people who think that their religion, their political doctrines or their morality are what make up their personality; they even segregate themselves from people who do not have the same values or try by all means possible to convince them of the truth of their schemes of thought.

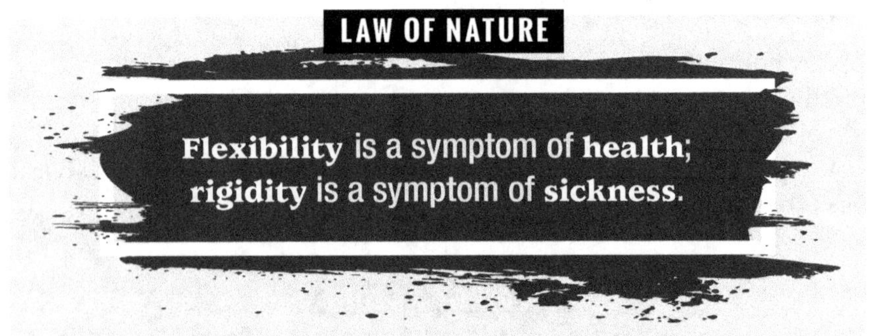

Identity 6. I am my hypotheses.

These people believe that they are worthy if their opinions or their vision of life are accepted by others. This is why people with this type of identity always want to be right and are in a constant power struggle. They believe that if they fail to be right in an argument or if they are wrong, they lose their value as a person. This is another example of an identity that operates on the plane of having.

Identity 7. I am my data.

Facts, laws, cause and effect— the verifiable—are the factors that define such people. They require hard data to define their identity. The typical thinking of people with this type of identity (which operates in *having*) is "if I don't see it, I don't believe it."

Identity 8. I am my being.

These are people who discover what they are and who feel worthy, regardless of the outside world, of what others think of them, of what others do, of their successes, of their failures, of the activities they carry out, of their changing values change, of their hypotheses and their hard data.

"I am myself, and the rest (money, health,
human relations, work or success)
are all tools to express my being."

It is important to point out that these mental maps are above all tools to observe ourselves, not to judge others. They are tools to generate reflective thought and compassion towards ourselves and others, not to label.

The more reflective thinking we generate, the more we can contribute to the world and the more compassionate we will be.

The experience of being a
human being is a challenge.

The names of life

When she was little, everyone called Maria de Jesus Lupi. Her family was quite well off, with no financial problems but with great emotional dysfunction due to her parents' infidelities, to violence, abandonment and loneliness. The girl was part of her family system, but in a state of total **unconsciousness**, she only felt fear and anger in order to survive. Even therapy didn't help her.

At the age of 17, Lupi decided to become María and, under the pretext of studying at the university, she left her home, city and country in order to leave her problems behind. So, she lived alone and was in a state of **rebellion** against everything that happened to her. She again had brushes with violence, and denied her origins and her parents. She had a car accident, an abusive romantic relationship, eating disorders and addictions. She was still in therapy.

When she finished college, at age 23, she hit bottom, fell into depression, entered a phase of paralysis and started calling herself Guadalupe. Depression left her in apathy and with a sense of victimization. She blamed others for everything. She was looking for relationships that would rescue her, but she felt shame. She didn't abandon therapy, but she didn't have the maturity to take advantage of it and understand it.

At 28, she decided to get a master's degree in Human Development because she liked the subject, but also because she was looking for

personal tools. She studied and learned ways to understand those tools cognitively; yet she still couldn't fully apply them to her life. She lived in **falsehood**, being an expert in the human psyche, but unable to transcend her own experiences. However, she was beginning to take action. Also, she always liked acting, and practiced it professionally. She had no money; was in toxic relationships and codependent.

Up to that point, she was doing what she could, without being intentional.

Maria was offered a very good artistic contract and took it under the pseudonym of Magú. But her colleagues did not hold up their end of the deal, and Maria had terrible experiences in a banal and shameless environment. But this made her react, and woke her up. She decided to end her artistic career and anything that was not based on truth and love. She eliminated toxic relationships and excess, and entered a phase of **courage** that give consistency and coherence to her life.

She began to give free workshops on Human Development and to reassess and understand all the tools that therapy and her studies had given her.

After a few years, at the age of 36, her workshops became quite famous, and she began to offer them at companies' headquarters. She became a coach, and her career took off. She re-evaluated her whole life and finally began calling herself María de Guadalupe, her original name. Today, she lives in gratitude for her life—her present one. She has forgiven everything and everyone—and herself.

Now she seeks **enlightenment**,
working hard from love. She knows it's
difficult but isn't afraid anymore.

Activity

This exercise is made up of two sections. First, answer the following questions as honestly as possible and without thinking about it too much; next, interpret the results based on the guide bellow.

Questions

1. Think about a person you admire and make a list of his or her five main traits.

   Examples:

   - *She's authentic.*
   - *She's natural.*
   - *She plans her things and organizes them well before taking action.*

   - *She's able to balance between her family life and professional life equally.*
   - *She's an international success.*

2. Think about a person that you dislike and make a list of his or her five main flaws:

   Examples:

   - *She's controlling; she likes to give orders to everyone.*
   - *She's quite afraid of being alone.*
   - *She has a big ego; she thinks she's better than she actually is.*

   - *She has a lot of arrogance; she doesn't listen.*
   - *She dresses terribly but feels she is a delight.*

3. Think about your biggest love, someone you currently love or wish to love, and make a list of his or her main traits.

    Example:

    - *He's kind-hearted; he has noble feelings.*
    - *He's very intelligent and sensitive.*

    - *He's nice to people and everyone loves him.*
    - *He's fun and always smiling.*
    - *He's resilient and strong.*

4. Think of a fantastic, adorable boy or girl. The child can be real or imaginary. Write five of his or her main traits.

    Example:

    - *She's physically beautiful—so cute that everyone turns around just to look at her.*
    - *She's nice; she's charming.*

    - *Very intelligent. Fast as a bullet.*
    - *She's loving and affectionate.*
    - *She's transparent and authentic.*

Interpretation of results:

The traits that you wrote below each question can reveal aspects of your own identity. What we perceive in others are usually a series of projections of ourselves; what we accept and love about ourselves—and what we reject and wish to hide.

- **Question 1.** This is what you love about yourself the most. This is generally what's found at the *public area* in the Johari scheme.

- **Question 2**: This is what you love the least about yourself. This generally belongs to the *hidden area*.

- **Question 3.** This is what you need to develop in order to empower yourself. It can be correlated with the *blind area*.

- **Question 4**: This is your essence—what you consider the highest features to have. This is how you express your essence. This can be corelated with the *unknown area*.

10

EMOTIONS OF
CONTROL

Emotions, as we have already seen, come as energy. Just like anything that is in constant movement, emotions naturally flow and change. The next scheme, entitled the Physiological Model of Neurolinguistic Programing, permits us not only to understand another way to classify emotions and identify them with more clarity, but also allows us to know how emotional cycles function in a natural state.

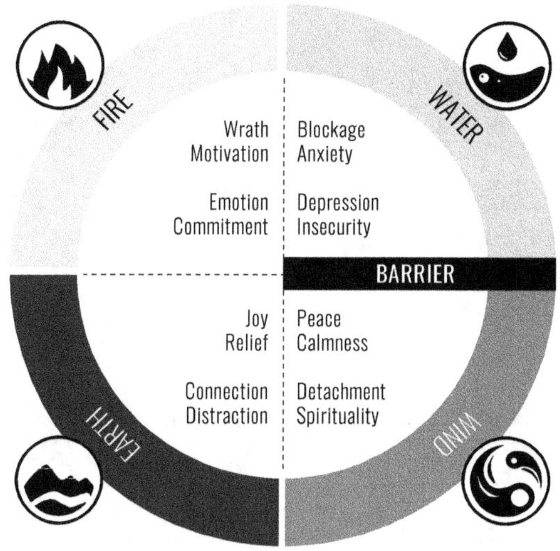

Water

Anxiety, depression, desolation and blockage are the emotional states related to this quadrant. Even though these are intense and reactive states, they are natural when something unexpected happens to us when we feel we don't know how to navigate this the challenge. It is natural to feel you're in a state of Water at the beginning of a crisis.

Fire

Anger, excitement, motivation and the commitment to change are the emotional states of fireworks. These are also states of high intensity. Once we accept the crisis that we are going through, two alternatives emerge: we either refuse the experience and get mad, or we don't get motivated to carry out the necessary changes to meet the challenge.

Earth

Joy, connexion, relief, and even amusement are typical states of Earth. Once we make the changes that were required by the previous phase in order to overcome the crisis, it's natural to feel emotions that, even if they are less intense, can be experienced as more comfortable. In this phase it's necessary to carry out the last adjustments to maintain the changes we already learned.

Wind

Peace, detachment, spirituality and fulfillment are the states of Wind, and only happen if we manage to convert our learning into a new lifestyle or a new personality. It is only possible to reach this state if we transit the three previous phases successfully.

It's only possible to reach to the
Wind phase if we are ready to accept
the responsibility of our Water,
Fire and Earth experiences.

It's important to emphasize that all crises or challenges of life imply transiting through each one of these states. There's no possibility of skipping any of them, even if a particular situation makes reaching Wind almost immediate, or if the process is slow. The only way to skip from Water to Wind, without passing through the other states, is by using some substance that alters consciousness, such as drugs. The big disadvantage of using drugs to reach Wind artificially is that people become dependent on a substance to generate the state—they lose their power, and worse, the state of Wind proves not to be sustainable throughout time, even if you develop an addiction.

Broken cycle

At times, either consciously or unconsciously, we remain blocked in a quadrant, especially in Water or Fire. We prevent the natural flow of emotions, and then **emotional blockages** happen.

If we don't identify and unlock the emotional knot, in addition to the physical symptoms, reactive patterns will appear in time. These are known as **"red buttons,"** which are people or situations that call forth the worst parts of ourselves. Emotional knots also explain obsessive patterns of thought, for example, not being able to stop thinking about the things we could have said, or how we could have defended ourselves during a discussion.

Not only do **emotional blockages** generate **red buttons** and patterns of obsessive thought, but often they are the causes of most of our physical uneasiness. Often, for example, what lies behind a muscular contraction or sore throat is in fact an **emotional blockage**.

It isn't our job to judge our emotions, nor to question why the natural cycle implies two states (Water and Fire) which tend to be uncomfortable. Our responsibility lies in making sure our emotions flow without obstacles, both when a new event detonates a new quick cycle, or when a cycle takes some years to conclude.

When this process flows, our energy looks and feels harmonious and expansive.

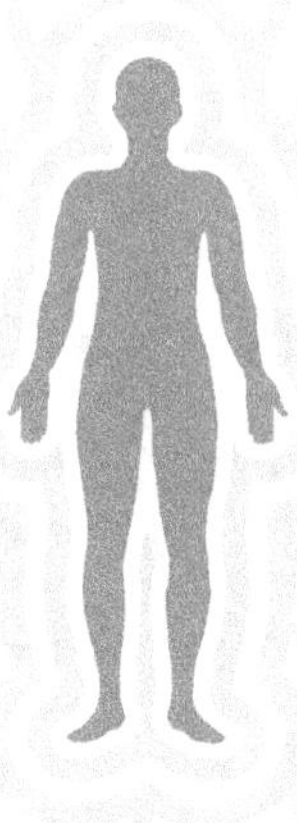

If we don't understand our natural processes, we are destined to get stuck. Then the electromagnetic field around our body won't flow, and instead will cloud our body due to emotional blockages, like a chaotic whirlpool.

When we're unable to identify emotional blockages and free ourselves, the more they keep obstructing our emotional *plumbing*, making past emotions get clogged at that point.

Consciusness centered on the being

Emotional blockage begins with a specific type of thought known either as a **tunnel thought** or **thought centered on the object**. They are a sort of a *waterfall* of thoughts that are fixed on something or someone external. It is true that this *waterfall* can be positive or negative, but it also tends to be generated much more strongly towards things or people that we perceive as threats.

When we experience these thoughts centered on the object it is as if our mind was an untameable horse. It doesn't matter how much we may pull its reins to place our thoughts on something else, the mind refuses and comes back again and again to the same subject.

Just like emotions, thoughts are
also designed to move, to flow.

Each time we feel we may not have the capacity to *let go*, making our mind focus more than the usual on something in particular, an internal alarm turns on. This alarm tends to be an adrenaline dose that our body sends, telling us to move and perhaps helping the mind to move as well.

Often, with all the adrenaline, rather than moving our mind, we drown even more in our tunnel thought, and the obsession with the object or the person that threatens us gets worse. It creates a vicious circle—more adrenaline, more *waterfalls* of obsessive thoughts.

When our body, that great companion of ours, sees that we are mentally blocked, it segregates more hormones (besides adrenaline, cortisol, for example), trying to provoke more energy to help us to move. But if we still don't listen to our body, then as a mode of protection an **emotional block** is generated. It's as if the mind has convinced itself at that point that whatever the threat may be, it is certainly stronger than we are, and hence requires a blockage in order to defend itself.

People who have been *stuck* with thoughts centered on the object for a very long time tend to become jealous, vengeful, excessively competitive, or obsessive.

The opposite of being centered on the object is to be centered on the *being*. Those who are centered on the *being* live free and fulfilled. They have the capacity not to judge experiences.

Things are not good or bad—they
just are, here and now.

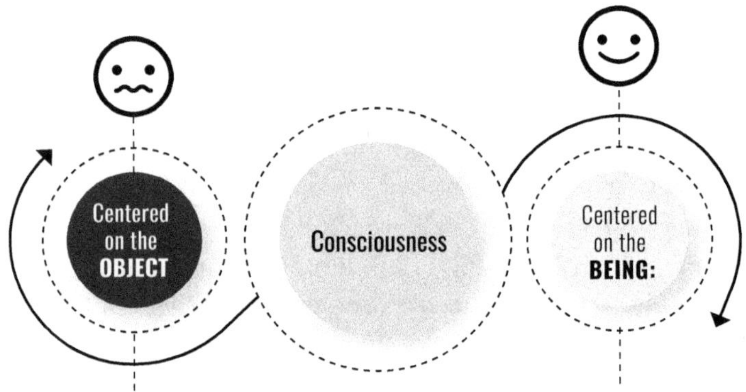

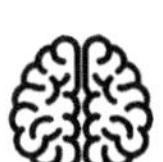

- The objective of my life is to not allow anything to interfere with my blockages.
- The belief that the world is a dangerous and hostile place. I must not trust anything and I must fight against everything.
- Those who touch my blockages are the cause of my problems.

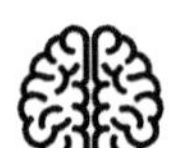

- It is understood that the nature of life itself is changeable and impossible to control.
- Situations in life are opportunities to undo blockages.
- It is understood that fear is the cause of all our problems.

- Emotions: jealousy, vengeance, competitivity and possession
- Weakness and insecurity

- Freedom, fulfillment, certainty

- The mind is usually used with the purpose of not fearing, feeling that everything can be predictable and definable. You want everything to be convenient.
- Long-term resentment

- Detachment. Things can be reasoned without judging and we can easily let them go.

The Blue Mustang

It's 5 a.m. A wonderful day is expected. Sandra exits her house, gets in her car and drives along *Insurgentes* to the south, towards Cuernavaca.

The sun shines. Every single thing on the highway seems brighter than usual. Sandra is happy because she is on her way to visit her fiancée. The radio is playing *I'm so excited* by The Pointer Sisters; Sandra sings the chorus once and again; she shouts it and dances it while the landscape passes by her window.

All of a sudden, after a blue Mustang has driven by in the opposite lane a thought strikes Sandra. At such a high speed it was impossible to distinguish the driver's features or those of the person sitting beside him. However, Sandra *feels sure*, without any sort of evidence, that the driver is in fact Rodrigo, her ex who cheated on her with a blond woman who was ten years younger than him.

In an instant, that perfect day becomes a terrible one, as if a storm cloud threatened to make her happiness collapse.

"It had to be him. How many tacky people would paint their Mustang with such a ridiculous color?" she began saying to herself while hitting the steering wheel with tears misting up her sight. "Yes, yes, and that damn blondie in his car must be the same one he cheated on me with."

Still, something in her mind told her that was not possible. They were going way too fast to be recognizable. No way could she have determined that it was the same blond woman. And the driver seemed too old. However, Sandra's emotions were blocked by memories of that bad experience, to the point where she threw away everything that had been making her feel good up to that moment.

Total eclipse of the heart by Bonnie Tyler was coming out of the car's speakers while Sandra wailed. She was crying and hitting the steering wheel again and again.

In a blind and emotional split second, Sandra violently turned the wheel to change directions and follow that blue Mustang. But she did so with such little skill that she ended up in a muddy canal right by the highway. Not only was her car now in bad shape, she could have killed herself.

After a while, the tow truck arrived, and moments later, her boyfriend Juan was there too.

"Are you okay?"

"Of course I'm not okay!" she replied with an aggressive tone, "How could I be okay if all men in the world are the fucking same!"

Juan kept a poker face, without realizing that his girlfriend's emotions had been blocked by her chasing a blue Mustang.

On her way to Cuernavaca, Sandra could have had a fulfilling experience. However, instead she experienced the pain and anger that she had never worked out. She hadn't become conscious of nor released her emotions from years ago, and on that day they were spoiling her life.

If we don't work on an emotion, it will remain in our way and in our mind, even forming an emotional blockage that will drag on for years, unless we choose to accept to be responsible for them.

Here are two exercises that can help us let go and achieve detachment in the face of certain situations or things that generate emotional blockages.

Consciousness exercises

On your phone, set up three different alarms during the day. Every time you hear it, ask yourself:

1. How do I feel? This is a check to detect anger, sadness or other low-frequency emotion.

2. Into what object am I pouring my consciousness?

3. Is it worthwhile for me to keep wanting to control?

Thorax breathing

Whenever something occurs that generates an disagreeable emotion, open your solar plexus with your arms behind you and begin "thorax breathing." This breathing consists of mentally counting four counts as you inhale, four counts as you hold your breath, four counts as you exhale, and once again four counts as you hold your breath. Repeat this process as many times as possible until you feel relaxed.

11

TO CONTRIBUTE

Any action that does not genuinely come from growth or contributing does not generate development or empowerment. It is merely an unintelligent action that perpetuates our ego systems.

It is important to point out that giving is not always contributing. Giving our free time to any altruistic cause, for example, is not necessarily a contribution. Deep inside it could be an attempt to demonstrate something (showing others that I'm generous), or participating in an association just because all my friends are part of it.

Interdependency

There are three ways we can relate with others and with ourselves. Ideally, these three ways of relating are synchronized with three different psychological phases which develop along with physical growth.

Nevertheless, it can happen that a person grows physically without having evolved his or her psychological maturity. Thus there are people with adult bodies, but with teenage or childish ways of relating to people.

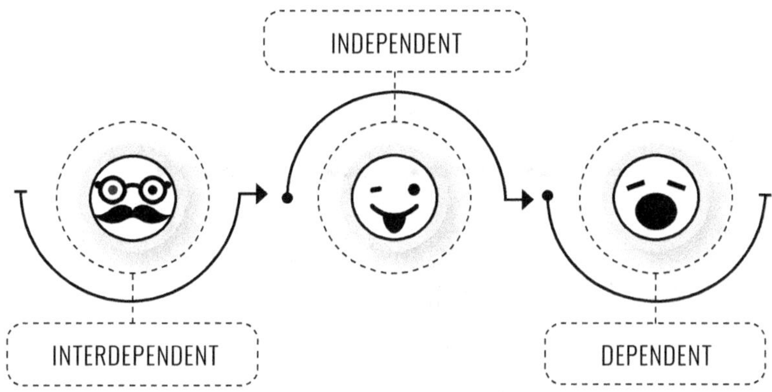

- The **independent** phase begins when a child is 2 years old until adolescence. It is characterized by the individual needing to demonstrate that he or she is independent, especially at the cognitive level. The individual tries to forge an identity, since until then he or she has confused his or her own personality with that of his or her providers. So in the search for this separation they need reaffirmation. In teenagers, rebellion, power struggles and drastic mood changes appear.

- The **dependent** phase is related to early childhood. It happens when a baby can't satisfy his or her basic need to survive. This means they need someone else to take care of their nourishment, shelter, affection, etc.

- The **interdependent** phase is the understanding that the adult individual, despite having the autonomy to achieve certain things, is immersed in an environment which makes them dependent on other people. Their achievements are always the products of a shared effort. In this phase, the person honors his or her effort equal to that of the others who made the achievement possible. In addition to being capable of appreciating that, without the help and presence of others, those achievements wouldn't have been possible, the person seeks to bring value to others because he or she knows that the growth of others promotes his or her own growth.

Although these phases are associated with phases of biological growth, most people with an adult body remain stuck in earlier psychological phases.

The average age for reaching
emotional intelligence around the
world is about 3 years old. In Mexico,
the average is 4 years old.

Emotionally, most adults are children who are seeking acknowledgment and want to show that everything should be credited to them. Egotism, corruption, being spoiled, machismo and toxic relations are some examples of adults psychologically stuck in adolescence, right in the **independence** phase.

To use

The only true way of giving is living in a state of **interdependency**. To give from the dependent or independent phase doesn't generate a real contribution nor an added value. That's because in these two phases all relationships are utilitarian—I use you and you use me.

How to know if we are contributing

In order to guarantee that a relationship is not based on using people, it is necessary to guarantee that those involved can also grow and develop. If a relationship holds up, hinders or interrupts the growth and fulfillment of anyone, it is a utilitarian relationship. Therefore the people involved are not contributing at all.

> If anyone is affected negatively, we are giving in a dependent or independent way.

Dependent

This is when we utilize **suffering**, in an unconscious way, as an exchangeable token in order to later charge for what we are giving. This is giving for the sake of an obligation or because we expect a later payback. It is done by emphasizing the sacrifice that our giving implies.

Interdependent

Here, not only is nothing is expected in exchange, but the mere fact of giving is gratification.

If the receiving shows they are thankful, if he or she squanders what is given, or is even hostile, it doesn't matter to the giver; the act is concluded at the moment of giving.

People who give in an interdependent way don't do so with a utilitarian goal. And they listen without judging. This person gives what he or she has, not what's left over. That act of giving also includes being generous with ourselves.

People who practice the form of Jewish mysticism called Kabbalah used to say that it's not a matter of desiring to have, but desiring **to share**.

To take intelligent action causes fear and pain and requires effort. And intelligent action demands from us what we don't have, but it generates a contribution.

Habitual action doesn't make us feel fear or require effort. Instead, it is comfortable, and we can give leftovers. But habitual actions always lead to the same place—without generating a contribution.

All of this can be applied to decisions
we make each second, not only
to seemingly huge decisions.

To forgive is the best example of giving. Forgiving someone who harmed us takes a lot of work, and there is pain involved.

In order to really forgive it is necessary to be in **interdependency**, and in that way, develop the awareness that no aggression is personal, even though it is directed towards me and has my name. Whoever attacks someone does so because his or her emotional system is dysfunctional.

Of course, aggressors are responsible for their actions, but being conscious allows us to understand that behind these actions there is a dysfunctional system. To remain in a victimization and complaint mode does not contribute, does not add value and wears us out.

Contributing is possible
when we understand people,
systems and circumstances in
an **interdependent** way.

Who to vote for?

Three candidates for a public position. Three men with many years in politics, but whom should one vote for?

1. Juan, (Dependent Party of Mexico)

He is a little childish, likes to joke around and always laughs at the physical defects of his adversaries. He asks for donations instead of working to satisfy people's needs. He collects favors and hired journalists. He's vain; he always buys the best suits and is known as Juan the Hunk. His political platform is based on the most radical type of populism.

2. Pedro (Independent National Party)

He shows fake leadership, claims he can solve all problems by himself, including building or destroying walls. He claims that his country is self-sufficient. He can't stand criticism. He refuses to look at international situations, because he says they are external, and that there is enough of everything for everyone in his country. "Do whatever you want" is his campaign motto.

3. Fernando (Independent Party of Truth)

He knows the potential that his country has, but is also aware that he lives in a global reality, and that it is not isolated. Not only does he have good ideas, he also accepts it when someone has better ideas than his. He thanks his critics as something to nourish his platform. He pushes for growth and, although he has goals, he knows that his are not the only ones. He advocates for just measures without being permissive or radical. He helps without asking for votes in exchange. He knows that if he loses, he will need to adjust the machinery.

Who would you vote for?

A good way to predict what will happen
in the future, is to observe how the
adult, the group, the organization or
the country relates an adult relates to
others in the present. If the relations
are in a dependent or independent way,
the results will probably not be optimal
in the short, medium or long term. The
real guarantee is interdependency.

Activity

Do this experiment in order to observe the way in which *you give* or contribute.

Observe yourself for a whole day. Before making any decisions, from the most habitual ones (when you brush your teeth, when you chose the clothes you'll wear, or when you decide what to have for breakfast, for example), to the transcendental ones (like having a difficult conversation with a collaborator, lending money to a needy person or choosing a new job), ask yourself:

1. Does my decision contribute to greater value to others as much as it does to myself, or does it only add value to myself?

2. Does this decision imply a conscious effort, or does it only keep me in a state of comfort?

3. Am I making this decision without even caring about receiving something in exchange, or am I making it just so someone else can give me something or recognize something about myself?

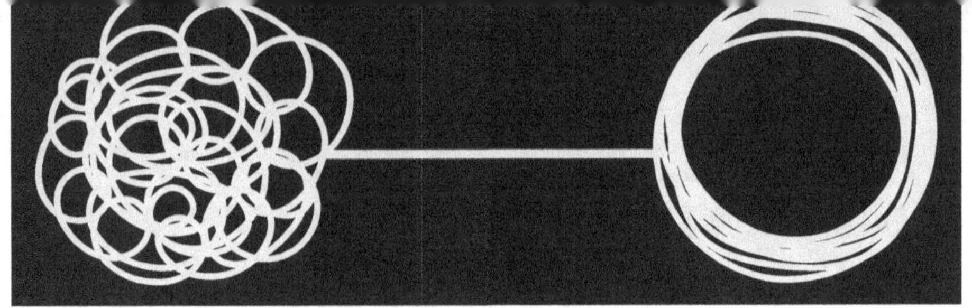

A story about reflective thought

The wooden boy

Since he was little, Pinocchio had always wanted to be a real boy. He always felt ignored, and why wouldn't he? At the age of 5 his parents had left him with an old Italian man, a carpenter and art restorer whose name was Geppetto. Mom and Dad never came back for him, so he grew up with the limited belief that he was not special in this world.

"I'm like a wooden boy; I'm just not real, nobody loves me," he used to think.

Although Geppetto would treat him with affection and give him everything he needed, Pinocchio couldn't stop thinking he was like leftover food. He was introverted at school, and his classmates would bother him because not only did he have a lack of character but he also had a big, peculiar nose.

When he reached middle school, his resentment was such that he decided to start lying and create a new personality in order to impress his new friends. He became an abuser, the same kind he despised during primary school. Thus, his limited beliefs generated a system of negative thoughts, which suddenly started to bring him unpleasant emotions. He felt wrath and sorrow and reached an explosive level of suffering.

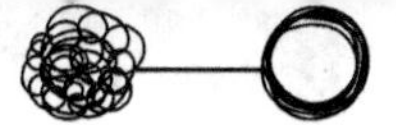

Soon the bad companions arrived, and Pinocchio changed into a total scoundrel.

"Once I was eaten by a whale, but I escaped and beat him up."

"You are lying! How is that possible?" his *friends* would say. They started to look down on him, but at the same time they respected him because he was the first one in line when it was time to commit an act of villainy.

Pinocchio felt his nose growing every time he told a lie, which would not only make him angrier, but also make him commit acts that were even more hostile.

He miraculously reached high school. His grades were terrible, but Geppetto had spoken to the director so Pinocchio could be accepted.

At the age of 19 Pinocchio befriended the meanest of students.

"I'm made of out wood, and I'm not afraid of anything," he would brag.

One sunny morning, a new girl appeared by the door. Her name was Morgan. She seemed like a beautiful fairy, with blue eyes and a beautiful golden head of hair. Pinocchio fell in love instantly. He would sigh every time she passed in front of him. The few times he tried to get near her, she would make a face and turn him down.

"It's surely because of my nose. But I'm made out of wood and nothing can hurt me."

However, Pinocchio felt his heart being squeezed after each one of her rejections.

"With that attitude of yours, she'll never pay attention to you. Even if you were the most handsome kid in school..." A squeaky voice distracted Pinocchio him away from his thoughts.

It was Pepe, a student who would always get the students together for art and meditation groups at school. Pepe would also set up strikes and incite students to participate in round table discussions to demand their rights be respected. That's why people would call him the cricket—Pepe the Cricket.

"Why so nosy?" answered Pinocchio and gave Pepe a thud on his head. "Gp on, get out of here!"

"As you wish, dude," said Pepe walking away.

There was a clandestine pool bar near school where Pinocchio and his friends would go drink beer instead of going to class.

It was late and the wooden kid was half drunk when he saw Morgan entering and holding another boy's hand. He was tall, handsome and a member of the school's honor roll.

"To hell with this…!" Pinocchio approached the couple and punched Morgan's boyfriend. But, since the handsome, sober boy was stronger, he was able to defend himself, and he gave the wooden boy a good beating.

Pinocchio went crazy. He broke a glass bottle, provoking a brawl which was followed by the arrival of the cops. All of a sudden, a savior's hand grabbed Pinocchio and helped him escape from the police, who were there to beat up and arrest anyone they could.

"Dude, do you really think that girl is going to pay attention to you? Forget about her. One day you'll mess up pretty bad, and you might end up in jail or worse."

With a hangover and feeling the anguish of not being able to win Morgan over, Pinocchio listened to that squeaky voice as if it was his own conscience.

Come with me," Pepe the Cricket said. "And if you don't like it, beers are on me.

Grudgingly and motivated by the promise of healing the hangover, Pinocchio accepted the invitation.

The place was a small studio and dance hall where some ladies who lived in the neighborhood had their Zumba classes in the morning. But at night, it was a place where guided meditations were held.

"What the heck!? What is this, some sort of sect? Are they gonna take my organs out and tell me about God?"

" Oh, quiet down. It's not that at all. You promised you would cooperate.

A woman placed herself in front of the group and began to talk about how to change beliefs which may lead to harmful thoughts, emotions, results and actions. Pinocchio felt something within himself being lifted.

After the speech, there was a meditation session that was meant to generate positive emotions. When the session had finished and almost everyone had left, Pinocchio approached the woman. Just before exiting that place, Pepe the cricket turned his head and saw how the wooden heart of his new friend had softened.

"I saw you crying during the session, Pinocchio, what is it that hurts you so much?" asked the woman.

"I won't stop fighting against the world. And I believe I've hurt others, such as my uncle Geppetto.

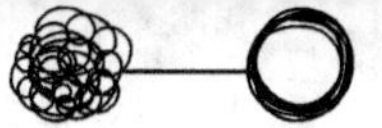

"Do you remember the subject we introduced tonight? About external and internal reality?"

Pinocchio nodded.

"Very well. What is that reality that you haven't committed to yet?

Pinocchio, as if Pepe the Cricket was dictating, replied:

"That I'm not good enough, which is the reason why nobody, including my parents, love me."

"And is that true, Pinocchio? Is it true that you aren't good enough and that nobody loves you?"

"No," the wooden boy replied as if something was still enlightening his answers. "The external reality I've been denying is that everyone, including me, is good enough. We are complete and worthy of being loved. That fear of rejection has made me behave this way. Nobody and nothing have really caused my behavior but me. Even what my parents did is possibly the best they could have done, and it has nothing to do with me or my value as a person."

And that was the beginning of a new path for Pinocchio, who would attend the sessions twice a week, developing the habit of meditating every day. Little by little he started to realize that the limiting belief of him not being important to the world was an obstacle that got in the way of his growth. His relationship with Geppetto strengthened, and his thoughts changed in order to generate actions that would make him congruent with the external world. He stopped fighting and drinking like a Viking. He evolved.

By the next school year, when Pinocchio arrived in the classroom he was almost completely unrecognizable. Pepe the Cricket was able to organize a collective dinner and Pinocchio participated, even though he wasn't interested in strikes at all.

Morgan broke up with her boyfriend. But despite Pinocchio's' attempts to hang out with her, she still didn't pay attention to him. She got a new boyfriend. The wooden boy didn't take it badly. He recognized the consequences of his previous actions and accepted the reality.

One day, the teacher announced to the group that there was a new student in the class. Her name was Azul. Pinocchio looked at her and fell in love again…this time with the certainty that he was no longer a wooden boy.

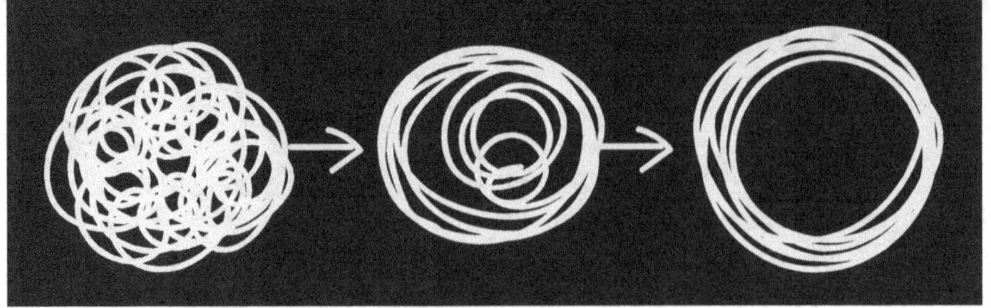

A story about emotions

Woe is me

"Woe is me, Llorona, Llorona..." The song, a traditional Spanish son about a sometimes-ghostly woman beset by tragedy and tears, played over and over in her head. The room was dimly illuminated by the light of dawn, perhaps the last. The woman in the bed lamented, as always, as ever.

"Woe is me, Llorona, Leonora..." the patient whispered on her sickbed, faithful to how she had always been: complaining, suffering, mired in suffering, never taking responsibility for the sad life that she forged herself. She still continued to blame others for her fate. "Oh, my children... Where are my children now?"

Leonora was born in the province of Seville during the second decade of the 20th century. Her small town was marked by the scars of medieval ruins and ideas that hadn't changed much since then.

She was beautiful. Her white skin contrasted with her black hair. Her features reminded everyone of the virgins in the temples, and just seeing her made you want to pray. Since she was little, her intelligence stood out among other children, although her strong and impious temperament often turned her beautiful black eyes into a well of bitterness.

Joaquín was the head of the family and he never looked favorably on Leonora's desire to go to school, to learn more than just to read.

One day there was a knock on the door of the family home. It was Eugenia, the village teacher, who explained to the patriarch that the little girl could not waste her gifts just raising children and washing dishes.

"I will commit myself to leaving everything to take your granddaughter to the city so that she can continue studying, so that she will be the first woman in town to look at the world with different eyes."

Joaquín's response was to slam the door in Eugenia's face. However, something of that proposal remained dancing around in the old man's mind. "One less mouth to feed... Maybe one day this girl will get us out of this poverty," he thought. But then he recoiled. "No, no and no. That would go against all my beliefs."

Leonora did not take her grandfather's refusal well. Inside the little girl, a monster began to grow that would accompany her all her life—because she had not only been denied the opportunity to learn, but also to control her strong character by way of an emotional education.

The little girl flourished. She became the most beautiful and coveted teenager in the region, so her grandfather promised her in marriage to one of the sons of the wealthiest family in the area. With that the old man was able to fulfill his dream of taking advantage of the girl, without giving up the limiting beliefs that tied him to his tradition.

Leonora complied with those patriarchal wishes, but her husband turned out to be a rogue, drunk, unfaithful and abusive. He only looked to Leonora to give him children—and to give her beatings.

That little monster inside Leonora was growing and infusing with it poison whoever approached Leonora, including her children—especially her children.

The years passed and every day Leonora blocked her emotions more. Her eldest son, fed up with his burdensome mother, left and nobody never saw him again. Her two youngest daughters put up with her because they had no other choice, until they got married at the first opportunity.

Leonora's anger escalated but she suppressed it. Suffering marked all her hours. She had problems with everyone, to such an extent that the children of the town gave her the nickname Leonora la Llorona—the crybaby.

Her husband couldn't stand her anymore, but her upbringing told her that she had to put up with him until death separated them.

One Christmas, Leonora's daughters and grandchildren came to the paternal home for dinner. But Leonora was rude, so that was the last time they celebrated Christmas with her.

After the death of her husband, the huge house she lived in turned into a tomb. No one visited Leonora, only the servants who reluctantly waited on her.

One day, while Leonora was walking through the town towards the church, a strong pain in her abdomen doubled her over and made her lose consciousness.

When she woke up, she was in a hospital bed.

"Cancer. There isn't much to do." That was the diagnosis that the doctor gave the servant—because Leonora had done so much damage to her children, that they were not there there to give her a helping hand.

"Woe is me, Llorona, Llorona..." The song played over and over in her head. Leonora closed her eyes, and strange dream invaded her mind.

Leonora saw herself, a girl again, running across the field as she had done before the monster inside her had grown.

"Leonora..." called a voice that seemed familiar to her.

The little girl turned to find the sweet face of Eugenia, that childhood teacher who, even in Leonora's old-age delirium, came to teach her another lesson.

"Leonora, child—you never knew how to channel your emotions. Your brain was a gift and you turned it into a weapon against yourself and against everyone because you didn't let go of the pain and frustration of not having been able to study and discover the world. But you still breathe, you can still forgive. Forgive yourself and take advantage of the great privilege of your intelligence by letting go of all the emotional blocks you have throughout your body, especially where you have cancer. There are a lot of knots, all tangled with the anger you didn't know how to channel. Perhaps that was your life's mission: to use your intelligence to learn to forgive, love and let go of emotions that no longer serve you. There's still time. Don't let your emotions and blocking of truth turn you into a crybaby until your last breath."

The dream seemed to last a long time, long enough for the girl-woman's mind to review her life. Then Leonora thought, in dreamlike incongruity, that Eugenia was slowly turning into a monster—into Leonora's monster.

"You are going to die alone," said the hideous creature. Then Leonora woke up.

"Paper... paper and pencil," the old woman ordered the servant. Leonora wrote a note and asked that they send it to her daughters, her grandchildren, to whomever wanted to read it. "But hurry, I don't have much time left."

"Please forgive me. I have already forgiven myself." This was the only sentence on that paper.

Days passed and there was no response. But just when Leonora thought she had acted too late, the door to her room opened.

Leonora thought she was dreaming again, because in front of her was a girl identical to herself when she was a teenager.

"I'm Maria, your granddaughter. And yes, I do forgive you."

At that moment. Eleanor smiled again.

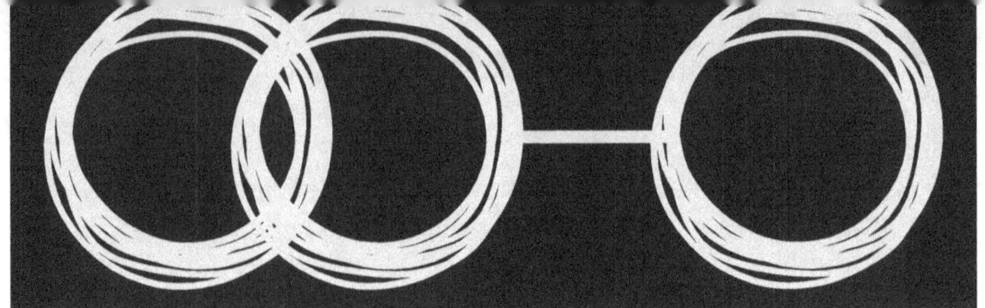

A story about taking action

The doings of pigs

Mama Pig had three children. The firstborn was big, strong and bore the proud name of his father: Cochino, which means "Nasty." Despite having great abilities, the first son of the family was laziness personified.

The second was named after his grandfather: Marrano, which means "hog," but he had inherited little from that famous pig. Despite being thin and skillful with his hands, he was lazy.

The youngest in the family got his name from a newspaper clipping that was flying around the day he was born; he was called Puerco, which means "Pig." The third son arrived as if brought by fate. Nobody expected him, but he did not feel bad about that. On the contrary, he was enthusiastic and analytical.

Following the family tradition, the three brothers studied architecture. Their diplomas hung on one of the walls of the family home; however, Cochino said that, as the firstborn, he did not need to build a house, since in the end he would remain with his father. Marrano was not willing to allow his older brother to keep everything, so he decided to remain at his parents' house to take care of the part of the inheritance that was his by law. Puerco, on the other hand, spent a large part of the day sitting in front of the computer designing plans for his future mansion, though he wasn't sure when he was going to finish.

Time passed and the three brothers were still installed in their comfort zone, until one fine day, Mama and Papa Cochino decided to have a very serious talk with them.

Sitting in the living room, the brothers faced the questioning gaze of their parents.

"Okay, you trio of parasites, your mother and I have made the decision to sell the house and go spend our last years traveling the world on a motorcycle."

Cochino, Marrano and Puerco were round-eyed; they hadn't expected their parents to throw them out and then hit the road dressed as 1970s *hippies*.

"So you guys have a month to find a place to live," concluded the mother, who was embroidering a skull on a motorcycle jacket.

Before the brothers could complain, the father spoke up: "I don't want to hear whining or complaining. We've already done enough to give you a career and support you for many years, longer than we should have."

Later, sitting in their room, the three brothers discussed the future. "They won't go traveling," Cochino said as he scratched his belly. Mom gets dizzy even at carnival rides. How could she endure hours and hours on a curved road?"

"And if they do go?" Marrano argued with a trembling voice. He was a nervous wreck. Where am I going to live?

"I guess we'll just have to use what we learned in college and build our own house." I've almost finished the plans for mine," Puerco boasted.

"You've been saying the same thing for years," said one of the others.

"An evil wolf is on the loose," said the newscaster. "This maniac, whose name is Feroz, blows down the houses of piggies and then sells their skin at a pork rind snacks plant."

The terrified brothers begged their parents not to leave them at the mercy of the butcher wolf Feroz.

"We're leaving," the piggies' parents said in unison.

The brothers had no recourse. The departure date arrived and, the three stood in the street, then set off to build their homes.

Cochino had the limiting belief that he could do anything (despite never having done anything in his life). He said that Feroz had done him a favor, so he gathered some straw, arranged it, raised some walls, put up a roof and finished very quickly.

"A cool house for this hot weather, like on the beach," he announced, full of himself. "I'm sure that fool Feroz won't come here. He knows I'm the toughest guy on the road."

But one cold night a howl was heard. Cochino got up scared when he heard it, knowing the wolf was nearby, but he told himself that he was an invincible pig and went back to sleep.

But soon enough came the hour when Cochino's actions, stemming from conceit and limiting beliefs, were put to the test, as Feroz filled his lungs with a mighty breath and easily brought down the straw house.

Marrano lived in anguish. His limiting belief told him that at any moment everything could go wrong, so he lived in fear, which led him to take action and build a wooden house. In the event of some shake-up, at least he wouldn't be crushed by his roof of straw.

When Feroz got there, he filled his lungs and blew once, twice, and on the third try managed to knock down the wooden house. Indeed, the roof did not crush Marrano, but his fear prevented him from moving and he there he was, paralyzed, when the wolf found him.

A little before he was thrown out on the street, Puerco had managed to finish the plans for his house. He also had limiting beliefs, but managed to change them when faced with the shock of finding himself without a place to live. He dug foundations, baked bricks, got concrete and even put in towers. He constructed a fortress.

When Feroz arrived, he blew and blew but soon got tired of blowing to no avail. Dead tired, the wolf fell to the ground—which gave the police an opportunity to capture him. They found him in possession of two lazy pigs that he intended to sell on the black market for pork rinds.

Puerco took his brothers in on condition that they change their beliefs and take actions leading to good results. Soon, the three brothers built a condominium where they received, to their surprise, postcards and photographs from their parents, who, by the way, already had several tattoos.

Moral of the story: It's impossible to be successful, and sometimes even to survive when, like Cochino and Marrano, our actions are driven by comfort and short-term thinking. Laziness is a habit—a habitual action, not an intelligent one. Fulfillment has never arisen from laziness and instant gratification.

Everything that flourishes and endures is based on effort. Sometimes the effort is physical, sometimes it is emotional, and sometimes it is both. We don't know when or how ferocious wolves will appear in our lives, but we know they will appear. The big bad wolves are those crises that come to help us engage a little more with external reality and to grow. But there is a huge difference between how people with a lifestyle based on effort and responsibility navigate crises, and how people who are habitually lazy navigate them.

This doesn't mean we should not enjoy life and that we must always live rigorously, with relentless strictness. The moral here is about incorporating effort and responsibility into our lifestyle, whether there is a crisis or not.